LORCA

THE POET AND HIS PEOPLE

BY ARTURO BAREA

Translated from the Spanish by Ilsa Barea

HARCOURT, BRACE AND COMPANY   NEW YORK

The quotation on page 82 from "Whispers of
Immortality" is reprinted by permission of the
publishers from COLLECTED POEMS 1909-1935
by T. S. Eliot, copyright, 1934, 1936, by Harcourt, Brace and Company, Inc.

CONTENTS

PREFACE

This book is not meant to be a work of professional literary criticism, biography, or historical research, for which I should not have the right qualifications. If I had wanted to fit the Spanish poet Federico García Lorca into the compartments of literary history, to explain his technique in academic terms, to trace the influence of Spanish poetic traditions and modern European currents in his poetry, I should have had to exploit, and in some points to copy, the work of scholarly experts and of intellectuals who knew him intimately. The task I set myself has another range and another level.

What I have tried to do is to bring Lorca's poetry nearer to readers, particularly non-Spanish readers, by showing how it reflects and transforms the world of the Spanish people to which it belongs. Lorca's work is profoundly and revealingly Spanish and at the same time universally human. Through the shape and color of the Spanish landscape, through the earth-bound idioms, images, and emotions of the Spaniards, Federico García Lorca saw and expressed the suffering and joy, beauty and terror, love and death of mankind. But it is not easy to understand his poetry without clearly recognizing the reality on which his imagery is built. And this reality is Spanish in every concrete detail. I have attempted to show the interplay of observed reality and creative art, which is the secret of Lorca's attraction for both illiterates and highbrows of his country. I have had to speak as much of the "background," of the Spanish people and their response to Lorca's art, as of this art itself, because I believe that one helps to explain the other. Perhaps this approach will also help non-Spanish readers to a fuller enjoyment of his verse, even when its beauty is dimmed by translation.

The quotations from Lorca's work that I use in this book are translations of an almost literal kind, done by my wife, the translator of the text, in collaboration with me. This seemed the best way, because so far I have not found any other English translation of Lorca's poetry which transmits the concrete core of his images so accurately that the foreign reader can share the poet's vision. It is impossible to transfer all the mental and visual associations the imagery conveys to a Spaniard into another language grown from another physical and intellectual world, but it is possible to attempt a translation in which the kernel of each image is preserved. It was more essential for my task to have a faithful transcription of the original than a more or less successful English versification. Some of my own interpretations of obscure passages are likely to be wrong or at least arbitrary, but I think I may claim that they are akin to the reactions of Lorca's Spanish readers, of the people to whom he spoke.

Many of Lorca's personal friends have written about him and their accounts do not always tally. There exists no extensive biographical study based on Lorca's letters and on documents. As far as dates are concerned, I follow

here the essay of Angel del Río in the monograph published
by the Hispanic Institute in the United States (New York
1941).

Federico García Lorca was born on June 15, 1899, in
Fuentevaqueros, in the province of Granada. His father,
Don Federico García Rodríguez, was a prosperous, well-
read farmer; his mother—his father's second wife—had
been a schoolteacher before her marriage. An infantile
disease, about which I have no concrete information beyond
the fact that it existed, delayed the boy's physical development. He was about three when he began to speak, about
four when he began to walk. A slight impediment in his
walk, though not exactly a lameness, remained all his life.
The biographical essays by Lorca's friends fail to agree
on the psychological effects of his early illness, but it is
reasonable to assume that they were far-reaching, even
though he was a gay and active "normal" boy. Because of
his ailment, his childhood impressions and emotions must
have been molded to an exceptional degree by the women
around him. Certainly Lorca's work shows his singular
faculty for identifying himself with the inner world of
women. His relationship with his mother and sisters was
intimate and close throughout his life. An old family servant, a peasant woman, left a mark on his imagination and
understanding of country people by teaching him folk
legends, popular figures of speech, and folk songs to whose
rhythm he is said to have responded even before he could
speak.

At a very early stage the boy Federico developed a
dramatic sense which found expression in his games, in
little plays he staged for village children, in the Masses
he acted and the flamboyant sermons he recited to an ad-
miring household. The extent to which all this was an

emotional compensation for his physical backwardness is
a matter of guesswork or interpretation.

Later the Lorca family moved from the village of Fuentevaqueros to the city of Granada, and Federico's adolescence was shaped in its peculiar atmosphere.

Granada is an isolated, shrunken town, provincial in
its society and superficial in its manners, but laden with
traditions which reach from Roman Andalusia through the
intricate civilization of the Moors to the brief flowering of
the Spanish Renascence and the long slow decline of the
later centuries. The town is full of an intimate, secretive
beauty, a beauty of old gardens and arabesques, hidden
behind blank walls and overtowered by the great hills.
Granada has its intellectual elite, its pretentious patriciate,
and its vigorous common people leavened by the gypsies.

In this town Federico went to school, in a college of the
Jesuits, and began his university studies. He was a student
of law, without putting his mind to it. It was the conventional university career for sons of good Spanish families.
What he really loved and studied was art: music, painting,
literature. He became a fine pianist and a disciple of the
great composer Manuel de Falla in his research into Spanish folk music. He went on a tour through Castile with
the professor of arts Berruete, and in 1918 published a
small book of prose sketches, *Impressions and Landscapes*,
as the fruit of his journey. Of the poems he wrote in those
years some were included in his *Libro de Poemas*, the first
book of verse he published.

Young as he was, he made an impact on the intellectual
life of Granada. He won friends among the older, acknowl-
edged leaders of art and thought, who recognized his
astonishing gifts, and he delighted the young people to
whom he read his unpublished poems or sang the old folk

melodies which entranced him. But he was never bound
to upper-class circles. His roots went deeper, both in town
and village. The colorful, fanciful speech of the ordinary
people influenced his verse at least as much as did the
Spanish poetic tradition, and it was their vision of life
which gave him his human insight.

The famous Republican jurist, Don Fernando de los
Ríos, then president of Granada's *Centro Artístico*, took an
active interest in Federico's development and influenced the
course of his life at several turning points. It was on his
advice that Lorca went to stay in the *Residencia de Estudiantes* of Madrid, in an atmosphere utterly different from
the self-contained tradition of Granada.

The *Residencia*, a quiet college on a hilly ridge over-
looking Madrid, the upland of New Castile and the distant
Sierra de Guadarrama, belonged to a group of institutions
founded and inspired by the greatest Spanish education-
alist of the nineteenth century, Don Francisco Giner de los
Ríos. There generations of intellectuals were imbued with
a spirit of free, detached scholarship and cosmopolitan
humanism, strictly opposed to the sterile obscurantism of
the official Spanish bodies. The men clustering around the
Institución Libre de Enseñanza and the *Residencia de
Estudiantes* were a progressive aristocracy of letters. Their
influence radiated to all sectors of Spanish academic, literary, and artistic life and penetrated, in an unobtrusive
"Fabian" way, into the secondary and popular education
which had been the greatest concern of Giner de los Ríos
himself. Thus exclusive intellectual sets were kept in touch
with wider currents, although the boarders at the *Residencia* itself mostly came from the sheltered upper or
middle classes and lived in a rarefied air, as on an island—
or in an English university town.

From 1919 to 1928 Lorca stayed in the *Residencia* whenever he was not back in Granada. There his mind ripened; his independent taste was tested by his contact with intellectual fashions. He published little, except one or another poem in literary reviews. A short play of his was staged, without success, in 1920. In 1921 his *Libro de Poemas* appeared. It was hardly discussed. On the other hand, the unpublished poems he loved to read to his friends became famous through his fellow boarders at the *Residencia*, many themselves poets or artists. Soon his name was a legend as that of a modern "minstrel" who preferred reciting his verse to seeing it in print. He had openly ceased to bother about a university career (though he took the trouble to get his law degree at Granada in 1923, as a purely formal gesture), and kept outside all intellectual cliques.

Yet the discussions and the experiments in dadaism, ultraism and surrealism among the young "vanguard" poets helped him to get his ideas about the poetic material in Spanish popular tradition into focus. His poetical transformation of gypsy chants and ballads, which is the fruit of those years, shows that he had learned from modern symbolist poetry, with its stress on the image instead of the narrative content. The cycle of the *Poema del Cante Jondo*, which Lorca wrote in 1921-22, when he helped Manuel de Falla to organize in Granada a musical festival of the *Cante Jondo*, the "Deep Song" of the Andalusian gypsy, appeared in print only in 1931, after rigorous revisions. It is a complement to his more famous book of gypsy ballads, the *Romancero Gitano*, written between 1924 and 1927 and published, with enormous success among the critics and the general public, in 1928.

A profound intellectual change, showing clearest in the

almost theoretical "Ode to Salvador Dali" (1926), and
in a memorial lecture on Góngora (1927), coincided with
a personal crisis in the year of Lorca's greatest popularity,
after the publication of the *Romancero*. He refused to be
labeled as a modern interpreter of the Andalusian gypsy.
He was experimenting with surrealist forms, influenced
less by the French theoreticians of poetry than by the pic-
torial symbolism of his friend Dali.

Once again encouraged by Don Fernando de los Ríos,
Lorca left Spain in 1929, for the first time in his life, and
went to New York. His passage through Paris and London
left no traces on him, but his meeting with the alien world
of an industrialized country had a lasting effect.

During his stay at Columbia University and in the Cats-
kills he wrote the series of poems published after his death
under the title *Poeta en Nueva York,* "Poet in New York."
On the way back to Spain, in 1930, he gave several lectures in Havana in which he tried, under the cover of a
lyrical style, to analyze the basic factors in Spanish tradition which were most important for his own art. After his
return home the whole character of his work changed. The
stage of intellectual experiments with surrealism was past.
So was the stage of direct exploitation of the folkloric vein.
In the tragedies and poems he wrote during the remaining
years of his life the fusion between the "popular" and the
"cultured," the emotional and the intellectual, grew to com-
pletion.

In 1932 Don Fernando de los Ríos, then Minister of
Public Education of the young Spanish Republic, launched
a venture which taxed all Lorca's sense of stagecraft and
knowledge of popular audiences. With official backing and
under the direction of Lorca together with Eduardo Duarte,
a traveling theatrical company, *La Barraca,* was formed,

mainly of students. The amateur actors carried the classical Spanish drama to the most isolated villages of the country, and a public of illiterates or semi-illiterates proved that the love of the theater had never died out among the common people. With *La Barraca,* Lorca also staged his own plays. In those years he poured his passionate feeling for the sufferings of his people into great plays, while his lyrical poems became more deeply personal than they had been before. He still had his spontaneous and infectious gaiety; it found an expression in the puppet plays he wrote with an enjoyment that speaks through every impudent phrase. He had not lost his sense of melody either; his settings of old folk songs were made famous by the singer Argentinita. But the concentrated power of his mature art went into tragedies and into a great elegy.

The first of Lorca's tragedies of the Spanish countryside, *Bodas de Sangre,* was put on the stage in 1933. It had a triumphant success not only in Spain but also in Argentina, where Lorca himself went as a lecturer and producer and was acclaimed as no other Spanish writer had been in living memory. In 1935 his dramatic poem, *Doña Rosita la Soltera,* and his second rural tragedy, *Yerma,* had their first performances. This was also the year in which Lorca's "Lament on the Death of the Bullfighter Ignacio Sánchez Mejías" appeared. He was preparing a cycle of poems based on Arabic verse forms for publication and had finished a new village tragedy, *La Casa de Bernarda Alba,* when the Spanish Civil War broke out on July 18, 1936. A couple of days before he had left Madrid for Granada, as he usually did during the hot summer months, though he, like everybody else, sensed the coming storm.

As far as the scanty reports make it possible to recon-

struct the facts, this is what happened in Granada. The
town and province were in the hands of Falangist and
kindred groups from the first day of the rebellion against
the Republican Government. Lorca found it necessary to
go into hiding because he was, though unpolitical, known
as a friend of left-wing intellectuals, an adversary of all
forms of reaction, and through his work one of the people's
party in the widest sense of the term, whether he wanted
to be or not. A writer who was a member of Falange and
therefore seemed able to protect him gave him a refuge
in his house. In the absence of this friend, Luis Rosales,
Lorca was taken away by an official or unofficial terror
gang. Rosales' attempts to rescue him on the same day
failed. Apparently he was shot with a batch of Republican
prisoners at dawn on the next day, August 19, 1936.

It took weeks before the outer world heard of the mur-
der. The new authorities ignored what had occurred, preferred not to investigate. Nothing is known of Lorca's
grave.

Tardará mucho tiempo en nacer, si es que nace,
un andaluz tan claro, tan rico de aventura. . . .

Much time will pass until there is born, if ever,
an Andalusian as clear, as rich in adventure. . . .

F. GARCÍA LORCA

THE POET AND THE PEOPLE

Those of us who were born in Spain during the eighteen nineties and became aware of the surrounding world just after the turn of the century found ourselves thrown into a society in permanent crisis. As children we came to feel, vicariously, the impact of all the shocks that racked our parents and their friends, many of whom defeat and poverty had made bitter and peevish. We grew up in a State battling against social rot and international inferiority, at a time when other European nations seemed on the road to lasting prosperity and security.

By 1898 Spain had lost everything: she had lost her short-lived hope of a republic which might have incorporated her in the democratic movement of Europe, and later she had lost the remnants of her American empire in the pitiful Cuban War. Thus crippled, she lived on usurious foreign loans for which she paid by handing over her copper and iron, pawning her railways, and selling her water power, to foreign owners. Spain was without an industry when the big modern industries were developing in Western Europe and the United States. Her fertile but mismanaged lands were exhausted, her crops reduced by annual droughts, while irrigation schemes and new methods of agriculture were futilely discussed; the country was short of bread. But it was plagued by earthquakes, epidemics, and floods which in the eyes of the bewildered, ignorant people heralded the Apocalypse. The monarchic regime with its rule of blustering generals or flashy "liberal" politicians smelt of decay.

The best writers, poets, and thinkers of that period strove to express their haunting experience of defeat, to explain and to overcome it. Galdós, Unamuno, Baroja, Valle-Inclán, Azorín, Machado became the leaders of a movement of intellectual and social self-criticism, known as the "Generation of '98." In the spiritual life of Spain it has left deep traces which nothing has yet obliterated and hardly anything overlaid. They established contact with the world outside Spain, only to return to the problem that possessed them, the problem of their country's inner life.

By the time the generation born in the years of collapse had grown up, bitterness and unrest had deepened; the foundations of existence had shrunk further; the criticism of the older rebels did not fill the void. There was a period reaching from the First World War to the late twenties, when the young people—my own generation and Lorca's—tried hard to live their own life, bright on a dark background, without wrestling with the problem of Spain as those others had done.

The lonely poet Antonio Machado, who belonged to the group of '98 in his concern for Spain, but to no group in his poetry, believed in our revolutionary mission. He thought that our generation would win that clean new life of which he only dreamed. In 1914—when Federico García Lorca was a boy on the verge of adolescence—Machado wrote a poem called "A Young Spain"; this is what he said of his youth and of ours:

[1] It was a time of infamies, of lies. They put all Spain,
our sorely wounded Spain, in Carnival mummery,
such as she was, squalid and poor and drunk,
that no hand should reveal and probe the open wound.

It was yesterday; we were but adolescents, when
in evil hour, pregnant with dismal presages,
we wished to mount naked on a chimera
while the sea, gorged with shipwreck, was asleep.

Behind us in the harbor we left the sordid galley
and pleased ourselves to sail forth in a golden vessel
towards the high seas, not expecting any shore
and casting overboard anchor and sails and rudder.

Even then, at the background of our dream—the
    heirloom
of a century that went, beaten and inglorious—
a dawn demanded entrance. Light of divine ideas
was giving battle to our turbulence.

Yet each one followed the set course of his folly,
limbered his arm, strove to display his mettle,
kept smooth his armor, shining as though it were a
    mirror,
and said: "Today is bad, but mine is the tomorrow."

Today is that yesterday's tomorrow. Yet our Spain
is still decked out in Carnival's dirty tinsel,
still as she was, squalid and poor and drunken,
but now with evil wine: blood from her wound.

You, younger youth, if from a higher peak
the spirit comes to you, will go to your adventure

    awake and limpid in the divine fire,
    clear like the diamond, like the diamond pure.

The poet of that "younger youth" was to be Federico García Lorca, in whose poetry the word Spain rarely occurs, who fought no conscious social or political fight, but who was so sensitive a recipient and transmitter of Spanish emotions that his work assumed a life of its own after he had been killed by unknown fascists, at the beginning of the Civil War in which he had no direct part.

There is no explicit political meaning in Lorca's work; he emphasized often enough, and rightly, that he had no politics. Whenever his writings express a social message it is on the surface unrevolutionary or even conservative. And yet he belonged to the Spanish popular movement for deeper reasons than that of having grown up to fame within and through the progressive intelligentsia of his country. Though he lived a privileged life in the charmed circle of Spain's aristocracy of letters, though he read his poems and plays first to young people coming from his own social caste, and influenced the rising generation through them, though he played and experimented with the most esoteric forms of modern art, he became not the poet of a "highbrow" set but a poet of the Spanish people.

A great part of his work is popular in the sense of touching his people as though with the full charge of their own half-conscious feelings, intensified and transformed through his art. The emotional forces he released became part of the shapeless revolutionary movements of Spain whether he intended or not. Thus it was, I believe, inevitable that he was killed by obscure fascist brutality and that his work became a banner.

It is of this Lorca that I want to speak first.

All Spanish intellectuals who have written about him have a right to say: "The Federico with whom I lived in the *Residencia de Estudiantes* . . ." "My friend Federico . . ." "When he read that poem to us . . ." "I remember Federico telling me . . ."

I myself never knew Federico García Lorca, though he was of my generation, a couple of years younger than I. I did not belong to any of the circles in which he moved. But I belonged to his public, the ordinary people of Spain, and it is the people's Lorca whom I know.

When the Civil War had become a war of the trenches, after the hot summer of 1936, and the news that Lorca was shot in Granada became known, *milicianos* who could neither read nor write learned his ballads by heart. The tunes and texts of the simple little folk songs he had revived became war songs of the Republicans.

The famous slogan "They shall not pass"—*No pasarán* —was used at meetings and in the press. But the soldiers in the trenches around Madrid preferred to sing the ditty:

> "Through Cuatro Caminos
> oh my mother,
> no one passes."

Cuatro Caminos is a working-class district of Madrid. The name means "Four Ways" and it fitted easily to Lorca's tune of the *Cuatro Muleros,* the "Four Muleteers." The militiamen sang the gay lines in which Lorca had recast an old folk song as often as they changed them to the "no one passes":

[2]   Of the four muleteers,
          oh my mother,
          who come to the water,

he with the dappled mule,
oh my mother,
has stolen my heart.

Of the four muleteers,
oh my mother,
who come to the river,

he with the dappled mule,
oh my mother,
has married me.

Why do you go for fire,
oh my mother,
why go up the street,

if your own face is burning,
oh my mother,
with the live flame?

I had a friend, almost illiterate, forty-six years old, in
the Republican militia from the first days of the struggle,
who sometimes came to my office in Madrid when he was
on leave from his post in Carabanchel, four miles away in
the southwestern sector of the front line. He would pro-
duce a tattered copy of Lorca's *Romancero Gitano*, filthy
with the grease and mud of the trenches, and say: "Explain
this to me. I can feel what it means and I know it by heart,
but I can't explain it." And he would recite the opening
lines of the "Ballad of the Spanish Civil Guard":

[3] ∨   The horses are black,
black are the horseshoes.
On their capes glisten
stains of ink and of wax.

Their skulls are of lead,
so they have no tears.
With their souls of patent-leather
they come down the road,
hunchbacked, nocturnal.
Where they breathe they impose
silence of dark rubber
and fear of fine sand.
They pass if they wish to pass,
and they hide in their heads
a vague astronomy
of incorporeal pistols.

I would try to tell him:
This is Spain—an enormous barracks of the Civil Guard. They are black, they, their horses, the horseshoes of their horses. Black means mourning. Everything in Spain is black. The Civil Guard are the keepers of this black soul of Spain. Their capes get stained with ink, the ink that runs out of the horn inkwells they use, filling in official reports which inundate Spain and stock her prisons. Their capes are stained with wax. Wax has dropped on them from all the candles in all the processions in which the Civil Guard went along to protect the precious jewels of famous saints. They are killers. It is their profession to use their rifles and to kill Spaniards. The Civil Guard have never killed any but Spaniards. Therefore their brains, their minds, their skulls are full of the idea of killing with the bullets of their rifles: their skulls are lined and choked with lead. How could they shed tears at the death of a Spaniard whom they have killed, with a bullet cast in the lead which fills their minds by day and night? Their souls are black, hard and glossy like leather covered with brilliant varnish, like the patent-leather of their winged hats. Two by two they

ride along the roads and over the hills, their brains clogged
with lead, their backs carrying the hump of their loaded
knapsacks. In each knapsack they have a horn inkwell so
that they can write a report on the dead, and a candle end
so that they can write in its light even when there is no
moon and can scan the face of the man they have just shot.
For they ride by night. They hide in the dark of the night
with their ink and wax and rifle, and wait in silence. They
aim at a man's shape in the moonlight and fire. Therefore
people walk on tiptoes wherever the Civil Guard go; they
fall silent and walk as though on rubber tires. And their
teeth chatter, a shiver runs down their spines, as when you
hear the crunching of fine river sand on tiles under your
steps.

"You know," my friend Angel would say to me, "while
I was still a boy I worked in Carabanchel, not far from
the place where our trenches are now. In the winter my
brother and I walked back at night when the road was
nearly deserted. Sometimes we heard the horses of the pair
of Civil Guards, and then we threw ourselves down into
the ditch until they had passed, and then we ran home half
dead with fright and told our father that we had met the
Civil Guard. . . . All right, but what I can't understand
is why after these verses, when you would expect this man
to speak of the Civil Guard and the people, of the poor
land workers the Civil Guard have beaten up and the workers they have shot—why he then suddenly starts saying:
'Oh, City of the Gypsies!' and tells you a story about Jerez
de la Frontera in a night of fiesta, when the Civil Guard
make a raid. Haven't the Civil Guard beaten up others
beside gypsies?"

Indeed, Lorca's ballad goes on to evoke the childlike
and dreamlike Christmas festival in a gypsy quarter: harm-

less, gay people playing at miracle making in an unreal city of their dreams, in a silvery, magical night, beyond the harsh laws of violence and want. Nothing could be more unpolitical and "unsocial" according to accepted rules. Nothing could seem further away from the sordid reality of the clashes between Civil Guard and laborers, which inevitably surge up in the memory of the common Spaniard struck by Lorca's merciless word picture of the men with the "skulls of lead." But this very incongruity harassed the reader, who had waited in vain for the great social denunciation, until it stirred him to a feeling of human revolt.

Once I asked my friend Angel to read out the verses against which he used to protest. He stumbled along, muttering comments between the lines.

[4] √   When the night came,
        night, oh what nighten night,
        the gypsies on their anvils
        forged arrows and suns. . . .

"Those *fiestas*, you know—good for children and maybe for gypsies. But we're grown up—"

        The Virgin and Saint Joseph
        have lost their castanets
        and look for the gypsies
        to see if they find them.
        The Virgin is dressed
        in the robe of a mayoress
        made of chocolate paper,
        with almonds for beads.
        Saint Joseph moves his arms
        under a silken cloak. . . .

"It is pretty, but what do I care about it?"

> Standards and lanterns
> invade the flat roofs.
> Hipless dancers sob
> in the looking glasses.
> Water and shadow, shadow and water
> at Jerez de la Frontera.

"Now I know what's coming. I know it well enough. The Civil Guard beat up the whole lot and kill some of them, just like that, without any reason. But what has that to do with us? There are other things they've done to hungry people—"

> Oh, City of the Gypsies,
> flags in all street corners,
> darken your green lights,
> the Civil Guard is coming. . . .

> Two ranks deep, they advance
> into the festive city,
> a rustle of evergreens
> in their cartridge cases.
> Two ranks deep, they advance,
> double nocturne of cloth.
> They fancy the starred sky
> a glass case studded with spurs.

> The city, free from fear,
> multiplied its doors.
> Forty Civil Guards
> entered to loot.
> The clocks stopped
> and the brandy of the bottles

took the color of November
not to be suspected.
From the weather vanes rose
a whirl of long screeches.
Sabres cut the eddies
which the hooves trample.
Through the darkling streets
flee old gypsy women
with sleepy horses
and crocks full of coins. . . .

"Can't you just see the charge of the Civil Guard? I
remember a strike—but then we knew after all what might
happen to us—"
He went on, unbidden, caught by the verses he read so
clumsily:

Yet the Civil Guard
advance, scattering fires
in which, young and naked,
imagination is seared.
Rosa of the Camborios
sits groaning on her doorstep,
her two severed breasts
lying on a salver. . . .
When all the roofs
were furrows in the ground,
dawn swung her shoulders
over a long profile of rocks.

Oh, City of the Gypsies!
The Civil Guard move away
through a tunnel of silence
while the flames ring you.

Oh, City of the Gypsies!
Who that saw you does not remember?
Let them seek you on my brow,
play of moon and of sand.

"Only, don't you see," said Angel after a pause, "he can't mean it just about Jerez de la Frontera and the gypsies. He makes you see and smell the Civil Guard, curse them, but—"

I answered: "Don't you recognize yourself and all Spaniards in those 'gypsies' whom the Civil Guard assault and torture?"

He offered a timid suggestion: "Do you remember the Sunday in July last year, the eighteenth it must have been, or was it the nineteenth, the day after Franco proclaimed the insurrection in Morocco? We all went out of town as if nothing had happened and we fooled around like children. I went to the Jarama to bathe and you went to the Sierra and were nearly caught in San Rafael, only you didn't know it at the time. Just like those gypsies—though I don't think gypsies are at all like he says. But anyhow, he makes me think of how the soldiers shot at us from the *Cuartel de la Montaña*. And since then it has been as if we were fighting against the Civil Guard all the time, getting nearly as bad as they are, too—but I can't put it into words."

This, I think, was the reason why this poem has made such a deep and lasting impression on the Spanish masses. Superficially the *Romance de la Guardia Civil Española* describes nothing but a brutal clash between a group of Civil Guards and the gypsies celebrating their joyous Christmas Eve festival in the streets of Jerez de la Frontera —"Oh, City of the Gypsies!" The common Spaniard, in his hatred and fear of the black riders who always hunted in pairs, would feel surprised and almost hurt that the poet, after his opening lines with their load of somber associations, turned away to the gypsy world. But after the first jolt he—the "common reader"—would suddenly identify himself with those childlike, dreamy gypsies at play, assaulted by the naked brutality of the State. The verses would make him feel the clash in his own body, even though normally he might consider the gypsies a useless, inferior, good-for-nothing breed. And the unpolitical ballad with its novel use of old words and traditional rhythms would stir up rebellious emotions.

It cannot be easy for the non-Spaniard to realize why and to what degree the Civil Guard of Spain had become the symbol for the oppressive force of a hated regime. And thus it must be difficult to understand how much Lorca spoke from the depth of popular feeling whenever the winged hats of the *Benemérita*—the "Well-Merited Institute," as the official title put it—cast their shadows over his verse.

Founded as a rural police, the arm of the civil administration, the Civil Guard was supposed to maintain law and order in remote villages and to keep lonely roads free from bandits. Its members were ex-servicemen and discharged N.C.O.'s schooled in the wars and willing to live in barracks with their wives and children. The whole body was officially under the Minister of Home Affairs, in practice under the orders and at the disposal of the civil governors of the provinces, and of their local henchmen. For generations, people in villages and small towns who did not belong to the ruling caste knew the Civil Guard solely as the powerful and ruthless instrument of the *caciques*, the political bosses, the landowners and the rural money-lenders. Under the monarchy it used to be taken for granted that at election time the commander of the Civil Guard in each village would arrest the men known for their opposition to the reigning clique; the secretary of the local administration would make out a polling list complete with the names of all inhabitants, including some already in the cemetery; and on the day after the poll the Civil Guard would release the arrested men. They hardly ever protested, for they knew the power behind the Corporal of the Civil Guard and had no wish to feel the end of his rifle butt. But they came to hate the Civil Guard with that bitter personal hatred which it is difficult to feel for an impersonal system. To them, the Civil Guard *was* the system which made them work for 1.50 pesetas a day in the olive fields: it was the men of the Civil Guard who shot at them when they dared to protest, and who beat them lame when they had the misfortune to be arrested during a strike. And they learned ruthlessness from the forces of law and order.

The "pair"—the two local Civil Guards patrolling the roads of the township—moved in this cloud of hatred and violence, and at their approach people shut their lips and averted their eyes. The Republic tried to build up its own police force, free from those associations, but the Civil Guard lived on, a sinister phantom, until it became a concrete part of Franco's Spain.

True to his own way of expression, Lorca never showed the Civil Guard as a social and political machine, at least not consciously. Yet even apart from the "Ballad of the Spanish Civil Guard," all his passing references to the *Benemérita* drew from the dark well of popular fear. He spoke of nothing but the traditional feud of rural police

and smugglers, public order and vagrants; but every encounter between his gypsies, eternally ingenuous, reckless,
and gallant even in their small vanities, and authority
embodied in the Civil Guard, became in his poetry a clash
between ominous organized violence and generous, gay
human freedom. And it was this underlying meaning which
Lorca's simplest readers felt more clearly and concretely
than his sophisticated public.

There is the "Ballad of the Brawl":

[5]   The Judge, with the Civil Guard,
        comes through the olive groves.
        Slippery blood groans
        its mute snake song.
        "Gentlemen of the Civil Guard,
        this is the same old story.
        Here died four Romans
        and five Carthaginians. . . ."

A good many Spaniards failed to understand the last
lines, with their reference to the traditional masks in the
religious processions of Andalusia, those legendary Jews,
Romans, Carthaginians in fantastic, stylized costumes, be-
longing to rival confraternities, who often came to blows
in drunken brawls. But all recognized the hard accent of
the judge-magistrate's "the same old story," and visualized
the chorus of the Civil Guard.

Then there are these lines in the "Somnambulant Ballad" of the mortally wounded smuggler pursued into his
last refuge:

[6]   The night grew intimate
        like a little square.

> Drunken Civil Guards
> were beating on the door. . . .

In the *Poema del Cante Jondo*, which Lorca wrote in 1921-22 and published, much revised, in 1931, there is the "Song of the Flogged Gypsy":

[7] ✓   Twenty-four strokes,
twenty-five strokes.
Later in the night my mother
will wrap me in silver paper.

Civil Guard on your round,
give me a sip of water,
water with fishes and boats,
water, water, water, water!

Oh, you boss of the Guard
up in your big room,
no silk handkerchiefs
will wipe my face clean!

To the Asturian miners who had escaped alive from police stations during the "Black Years" of 1934 and 1935, this cry of the thirst-tortured boy who dreams of drinking up the sea with its fishes and boats, who longs for the coolness of tinfoil and silk against his burning, lacerated skin, was stark realism and a call to action, not lyrical verse inspired by gypsy folklore.

During the first half of the Spanish Civil War the ordinary men and women who lived and fought in Madrid were driven by a multitude of emotions like these, not by thought-out reasons. Most of them felt no urge to hear about their miseries and sufferings, their wrongs or their rights, but they delighted in discovering themselves, in exploring their own feelings, faculties, and tastes. This made the trenches and factories so rich in individual creative acts, so rich in absurd or heroic initiative. This made Lorca so beloved, for his verses had the power to make people feel and see familiar things in a new, clear light.

My friend Angel once brought a soldier from his company in Carabanchel to see me. This soldier was a young man from Jaen, who had escaped the Fascists through the endless olive groves, marching through half Spain until he reached Madrid and was given a rifle. He never explained why he did it; he had to. He was a land worker, half Andalusian, half gypsy; his skin shone with a golden glow.

"I've brought him along so that you can read him something by García Lorca. He can't read himself."

The olive fields of Jaen . . . I read:

[8] √   The olive field
        opens and shuts
        like a fan.
        Over the olive grove
        is a deep sky
        and dusky rain
        of cold stars.
        Shadow and rushes shiver
        on the river bank.
        The gray air ripples.
        The olive trees
        are laden
        with cries,
        a flock

of captive birds
who move their long long tails
in the twilight.

"That's right. Look: If you stand in the middle of an
olive field between two trees, you look along a straight
lane, like a fan that's shut. If you go behind a tree, all the
rows between the lanes open up like a fan. And if you
walk between the trees there's a big fan opening and shut-
ting before you. And the olive fields are full of cries and
calls. The fieldfares come in flocks and make a great noise,
even in the night when they're caught by the darkness and
have to stay in the olive trees. Sometimes you'd think the
whole tree is alive with wings and tails. They're a nuisance,
too, they're so greedy. . . . Read me more."

This boy had gone hungry working in the olive fields.
He had fought for life or death between his olive trees.
But they were his trees, and Lorca's verse moved him in
his sheer physical love for the trees which had been his
life. Perhaps he would have been less shaken and exalted
by a description of the social tragedy of the olive fields,
of which there is no trace in Lorca, than by the vision of
the big silver-green fan. I know he went back to his trench
convinced that Lorca was "his" poet, and therefore a revolutionary poet (though I doubt if he would have used this
word aloud, self-contained as he was). Yet this poem of
the olive field was conceived by Lorca when he was very
young, in 1921, when he worked with Manuel de Falla,
the composer, and Ignacio de Zuloaga, the painter, to re-
vive Andalusian folk art in the *Fiesta del Cante Jondo*.

It was not, as might be and has been argued, Lorca's
assassination in Granada which made him so widely and

profoundly popular in Republican Spain. The process I
have tried to describe—that of Lorca's art touching and
releasing emotions which are individual and at the same
time so simple, ancient, and common to all Spaniards that
they assume the quality of mass emotion—turned a minor
work of his into Republican propaganda at a much earlier
stage.

Lorca's historical drama *Mariana Pineda* had its first
public performance in 1927. The military dictatorship of
General Primo de Rivera was nearing its end; the throne
was shaken; the public—not merely political groups and
progressive intellectuals, but the "man in the street," the
people clustering in cafés and bars and slum alleys—
demanded more and more loudly an official account of the
Moroccan disaster, until then adroitly glossed over. The
movement for a democratic republic and against the dic-
tatorial monarchy was gathering strength. Censorship and
repression were at work, with close controls of the printed
word and with clumsy brutality within the four walls of
police prisons and Civil Guard barracks. The mass of the
people searched for means of expression, and the simplest
words were given a double meaning. At that time the famous caricaturist Bagaría, prevented from publishing car-
toons, began to publish designs for needlework whose
esoteric meaning the public learned to decipher like the
secrets of crossword puzzles.

In this atmosphere *Mariana Pineda* was staged. The
performances of what Lorca called a "popular ballad"
were turned into public demonstrations. And yet, defined
in superficial political terms, this lyrical play has a reactionary rather than a revolutionary bias.

Its historic heroine was a woman of Granada who embroidered a Republican flag for a planned liberal insur-

rection against the absolutist reign of Ferdinand VII, in
the eighteen thirties. The police got wind of the plot, the
conspirators fled abroad, and the only concrete evidence
found was the flag embroidered by Mariana Pineda. She
was arrested and hanged because she refused to betray the
names of her associates.

In Spanish history Mariana figures as an active Republi-
can; to Catholic and Monarchist Spain and its offspring,
Falangist Spain, she is a dangerous revolutionary; to the
Democrats a political heroine. To Lorca she was neither.
This is his interpretation:

Mariana Pineda is blindly in love with Don Pedro de
Sotomayor, one of the leaders of the liberal conspiracy in
Andalusia. A widow with two children, she has sunk her
whole longing for a free, happy personal life into this
love for a man who, though enamored, puts his somewhat
vague political passion first. Because he wishes it, Mariana
embroiders a flag for his party, which does not interest
her despite her hatred of all human oppression. She helps
him to escape from prison and from the cordon drawn
round Granada by the King's Constable, the judge Pedrosa.
But she is not in tune with her lover's perorations about
the salvation of Spain; she, too, longs for it, but for simpler
reasons:

[9] I want to open my balconies wide, so the sun
     may strew the floor with its yellow flowers,
     and to love you, sure of your love, with no one
     lying in ambush for me. . . .

The news that their conspiracy is discovered, its head
executed, and Pedrosa on the way to catch them, drives the
conspirators gathered in Mariana's house to headlong flight.

They leave her to her fate, even Pedro, who thinks only of preserving himself for further political adventures. Mariana refuses to betray the liberals to Pedrosa and rejects his amorous offers, deeply afraid and yet hoping that Don Pedro will come back to rescue her or "to die with her." Even when she is sentenced to death she still tries to retain her faith in the people of her town and in Don Pedro: "You forget that before I die all Granada must die, that very noble gentlemen will come to save me. . . . You say they leave me alone? What does it matter? One will come to die with me, and that's enough. But he'll come to save my life! . . . It cannot be true! Cowards—who is there who would order such villainy in Spain? What is my crime?" She is told that Don Pedro has gone to England: "Why did you tell me? I knew it so well, but I never wanted to tell it to my hope. Now it no longer matters to me."

And then, in the face of the abject cowardice of the revolutionaries who leave her, the least implicated of all, to be executed as the only victim in the town of Granada, Mariana rises above her terrible disillusionment and becomes transfigured:

[9 cont.]
    I embroidered the flag for him. I conspired
    so as to live and love his very thought.
    More than my children and myself I loved him.
    You love Freedom more than your Marianita?
    Then I shall be the Freedom which you adore.
    . . . .
    My children's faces will carry a glow
    that neither the years can blur nor the winds.
    If I turned denouncer, in the streets of Granada
    this name of mine would be spoken in fear. . . .
    . . . .

Pedro, I want to die
for that for which you die not,
for the pure ideal which lit your eyes.

. . . .

In my last hours I want to adorn myself,
I want to feel the hard caress of my ring,
and to put my lace mantilla on my hair.
You love freedom above all things,
but I am Freedom itself. I give my blood
which is your blood and the blood of all creatures.
Nobody's heart can be bought!

She goes to the gallows with the words:

[9 cont.]

I am Freedom because love wanted it so.
Pedro, the Freedom for which you left me!
I am Freedom, stricken by men.
Love, love, love, and eternal solitudes!

That is to say: In Lorca's play the heroine of political
history becomes an unpolitical woman in love, with human
weaknesses and an essential dignity, who sacrifices herself
for "her man," wanting him to be both reality and ideal
worthy of martyrdom—very much in the Spanish tradition. The "freedom" which she embodies is not the political
freedom from reactionary bondage; it is the freedom of
the heart and mind, which is unattainable—"man is captive and cannot get free"—and at the same time real—
"nobody's heart can be bought." This human dignity is
violated by the political oppressor, but also by the cow-
ardly indifference of people in general. In Granada, on
the day of Mariana's execution,

[9 cont.]

   . . . there is a fear to make you afraid.

The streets are deserted,

only the wind comes and goes,

but the people lock their doors. . . .

Even worse is the betrayal by the men who speak of liberty and their will to die for it, but who then clutch at their miserable existence to the extent of letting the woman pay the price in their place. Pedrosa knows this very well, when he tells Mariana:

[9 cont.]

No one in Granada will show himself

when you pass by with your last company.

The Andalusians talk, but afterwards . . .

A drama which thus deviated from the idea of popular heroism and made the Republicans look ridiculous might well have met with hostility in the Madrid of 1927; it might have been taken up by the Right and used for its purposes. In a way *Mariana Pineda* was indeed not a success: it was too much a "ballad," too little "theater." Only the woman Mariana herself and the atmosphere of Granada, with its sharp winds from the mountains and its echoes of old folk songs, emerged clearly, while all the other personages of the play remained shadowy. But even so, Lorca's interpretation of the woman was sufficient to make it a plea for human rights, and therefore against the Right in that particular moment of Spanish history.

The Spanish public, which might have rejected the idea of a woman sacrificing herself for political doctrines (even for popular ones), easily understood the woman who sac-

rificed her life for the sake of love, the love which is human
liberty, and converted her into a political symbol. To quote
Stephen Spender, although out of context: "Poetry which
is not written in order to advance any particular set of
political opinions may yet be profoundly political."

Señora Pilar, the concierge of Number 9, would be given
a ticket to the play. She would look forward to hearing
the story of "that wicked woman who was hanged because
she got entangled in politics," and tell everybody, including me: "Yes, sir, well hanged she was. Who told her to
go and get all mixed up with those revolutionaries? Women
belong to their homes anyway." (Lorca knew this attitude
well. In the first scene one of the women says of Mariana:
"What do things of the streets mean to her? If she must
embroider, let her embroider dresses for her little
girl. . . . If the King is not a good king, let him be,
women shouldn't bother about such things.")

But then in the theater, the soft music of the verse would
penetrate to Señora Pilar, and she would begin to weep:
"Poor darling, they're going to hang her for that young
scamp who deserted her. And he a grand gentleman—of
course! If it had been my Nicolas now, he's a Republican
of the good old sort. Well, yes, he's a bit simple. But if
he knew they were going to hang me because I'd embroidered a flag for him, he'd knock the judge's teeth out
soon enough." And suddenly she would rise from her seat
—she was not going to leave Marianita alone, not she!—
and shout: "*Viva la República!*"

Scenes of this kind, more or less naïve but always spontaneous, occurred almost daily in the *Teatro Español* during the run of *Mariana Pineda*. Through a drama with an
antipolitical argument Lorca had stirred popular senti-

mentality and sentiment, and set them in motion in a very different direction.

And, though his play did not return to the Spanish stage, he had infused new life into a half-forgotten folk song. In 1947 the girl apprentices in a Madrid dressmaker's workshop sang an old song with a barrel-organ melody, of which Lorca had used two stanzas at the beginning of his play. They believed that the "Marianita" who was put to death for embroidering the "flag of liberty" had lived much nearer their own time, much nearer Franco's Spain. But they never doubted that she had lived, that she had died for her belief in freedom, and that hers was a sad but proud story.

Another of Lorca's unpolitical plays had a similar effect at a moment when, once again, the power of an oppressively reactionary administration was wearing thin and the currents of mass unrest were running deep. The poet himself was dismayed, as R. M. Nadal reports in his preface to the selection of poems by Lorca translated by Stephen Spender and J. L. Gili, and published by The Dolphin (London 1939): "The production in Barcelona in December 1935 of *Rosita la Soltera,* a comedy of middle-class life in Granada in the late 19th Century, was made the occasion of political demonstrations. Lorca was saddened and observed to a friend: 'I am no fool, they are making politics out of my *Rosita,* and I won't have it.' "

Whether he would have it or not, Lorca's work had its inevitable effect because of the very quality of his art which lifted frustrations and longings of the individual to a plane where their general implications became clear. And yet *Doña Rosita la Soltera* seems purest romanticism in form and subject. The poet gave it the subtitle "The

Language of the Flowers" and, as a *leitmotiv*, the ballad
of *Rosa Mutabile,* the "Mutable Rose":

[10]   When it opens in the morning
it is red as blood;
the dew dare not touch it
for fear of being burned.
It is hard as coral
and wide open at noon,
the sun stares through the panes
to see it glow.
When in the branches
the birds begin their song
and in the violets of the sea
the evening swoons,
it grows white with the pallor
of a cheek of salt.
And when the night is sounding
its soft metallic horn,
and the stars are rising,
the breezes gone,
on the border of darkness
its petals fall.

Doña Rosita, the spinster—*la soltera*—is the incarnation of this mutable rose. Her love, her faithful waiting,
and her hopeless aging fill the three acts of the play.

Rosita, an orphan in the care of her uncle and aunt (the
uncle keeps a specimen of the "mutable rose" in his hot-
house), falls in love with one of her cousins whose father
lives in America. When he is forced to follow his father
overseas he pledges his troth to her. Fifteen years later he
proposes in a letter to marry her by proxy, and she agrees

with joy: a blossom of the mutable rose, which her uncle
cuts for her, is still red. After more years of waiting her
relatives learn that the cousin is married to another woman.
They hide this from Rosita and keep up the deception for
years, pretending that her fiancé will come back and marry
her one day. Haunted by the cruelty of her set towards
any jilted spinster, she clings to the make-believe which
has become the shell of her inner life, the only reality existing for her. After her uncle's death she and her old
aunt are forced to leave their home, ruined, helpless, and
hopeless. There is no way out into life for Rosita. The
petals of the rose drop.

Within a lyrical framework, Lorca's melancholy comedy reveals the shoddy emptiness behind the façade of
Spanish provincial life. He re-created his own city of
Granada around 1900, but it was more than a regional
period piece that he gave. That asphyxiating atmosphere
of prejudice, bigotry, hypocrisy, fear, malice, and genteel
behavior, in which the unfortunate girl Rosita withers
away, was only too well known to the great mass of the
theater-going public. And Lorca made the people of that
society come alive, in all their mortifying, deadening way
of living. Among them he puts a woman of the people,
Rosita's old nurse; rough, crude, and sane, swearing at
the rich and upsetting polite fictions, she exposes the inane
pretentiousness of the others through her primitive, warm-
hearted courage. This nurse only follows the venerable
tradition of "comic" nurses in romantic plays; also the
story of the girl fading away in a decaying house is old
enough. Yet Lorca pursued his vision with such art and
human veracity that "The Language of the Flowers" became, against his declared intention, a satire on a mori-
bund provincial bourgeoisie and an appeal to the living

force of the people. Pure romantic art was turned into social action and reaction. In the Spain of 1935, when that declining bourgeoisie tried to stage a comeback to power and to keep the unruly popular forces in bounds, this meant a surge of political emotions which frightened the poet who had released them.

The result was the same whether Lorca faced the people as poet, playwright, or producer. The stimulus he gave helped to shape political consciousness in a way which must have been alien to his intention—and yet faithful to it underneath the surface slogans.

In the first year of the Spanish Republic of 1931, Lorca proposed to his friend Don Fernando de los Ríos, then Minister of Education, the creation of a popular theater group which should present classical plays and bring the Spanish drama to peasants and laborers. He knew that interest in the theater, in the spoken word, had never died out among them, but was kept alive in clumsy puppet shows at country fairs, or in the dramatic chants during religious festivals. With official support Lorca organized a traveling company of university students, which he called *La Barraca*. He licked the group into shape and imbued it with something of his own creative enthusiasm. *La Barraca* traveled the roads of Spain, pitched a stand in a village square, set its stage in a barn or a shed, and made bewildered land workers listen to the sonorous verse of Lope de Vega and Calderón.

But *La Barraca* became a political weapon. Those spectators, now for the first time in their lives moved by passion filtered through art, were the same people who put their hopes in the new Republic, who listened in their village tavern to the newly installed wireless, who dreamed of a school for their children and believed that in future the soil would nourish instead of starve them. The words of the classical drama merged into their present-day hopes. If the wicked nobleman of the play was punished because he offended a seventeenth-century point of honor, they identi- fied him with one of the señoritos, the sons of their own gentry, whom they had learned to hate.

The greatest revolutionary appeal of all the plays popu- larized anew by *La Barraca* was Lope de Vega's *Fuente- ovejuna.* It was written in 1619 and deals with an incident of the year 1476. Its story is simple. The overlord of Fuenteovejuna, very powerful as the Knight-Commander of the Order of Calatrava, robs, kills, and violates at will until the whole village (which still exists) rises and slays him. Isabel and Ferdinand, the "Catholic Monarchs," who knew him as one of the recalcitrant vassals perpetually at war against their administration, send a judge to the village. He subjects the whole village, including the chil- dren, to torture, but the answer to his question, "Who killed him?" is always the same:

> *Fuenteovejuna,*
> *Todos a una.*

> "Fuenteovejuna,
> All as one."

In despair, the judge takes his findings to the sovereigns. The villagers follow him to plead their cause, to ask for pardon and justice, and to swear fealty to the King and Queen. The rulers accept them as vassals and mete out justice to them.

The drama was originally superb Royalist propaganda, exalting the supreme power and authority of the monarch as the people's best protection against the feudal lords; it is an interesting illustration of the class struggle at the beginning of the modern age in Spain. And at the time when *La Barraca* played it under Lorca's direction it could have appeared as excellent Monarchist propaganda once again. But the Spanish monarchy had collapsed in 1931 precisely because it was incapable of meting out justice to "Fuenteovejuna," to the common people of the whole of Spain. The laborers in the villages recognized themselves in the men of Fuenteovejuna, but they did not recognize their late King in the wise monarchs of the play. The lesson which the drama drove home to them was that a mass acting together and at the same time, *todos a una*, becomes invincible.

Other seventeenth-century plays revived by Lorca's troupe had no such direct propagandist message, but, played as they were, they too had their social effect. I remember seeing an open-air performance of a cloak-and-dagger tragedy which *La Barraca* gave in one of the oldest squares of Madrid, with crooked little alleys opening into it. The play came alive with torchlights, balconies, and guitars, with cloaked gentlemen and astute servants, with a strict code of honor, complicated intrigues, sudden passion and sudden violence. It became a fascinating, repellent evocation of ghosts. There in the homely streets the public felt more deeply than it would ever have felt in a big modern theater that the world of the play was dead and ought to stay dead.

The work of Lorca the producer, as that of Lorca the playwright and poet, was part of the movement of the Spanish people.

The reasons went far deeper than a coincidence of atmosphere and historic moment; they were as deep as the

roots of Lorca's art, of which I shall have to speak. However distant from party politics and from obvious "Left"
activities Lorca kept himself, he knew very well what he
wanted to do for his people through the theater.

In 1935, at a special performance of his tragedy *Yerma*
in the *Teatro Español* of Madrid, he said in a speech
addressed to the actors and workers of the theater:

> Tonight I am not speaking as the playwright,
> or the poet, or the simple student of the rich
> panorama of man's life, but as an ardent, pas-
> sionate believer in the theater of social action.
> The theater is one of the most expressive and
> useful instruments for building up a country; it
> is the barometer of its greatness or decline. An in-
> telligent theater, well oriented in all its branches
> from tragedy to vaudeville, can change the sensi-
> bility of a people within a few years; a disinte-
> grated theater, with clumsy hooves instead of
> wings, can cheapen and lull into sleep an entire
> nation. The theater is a school of tears and laugh-
> ter, and a free tribune where men can reveal
> outworn or ambiguous morality, where through
> living examples they can explain the eternal laws
> of the heart and mind of man.

THE POET AND SEX

Federico García Lorca, who never wanted to face politics, did face the problems of sex with the greatest clarity. Now, sexual life has in every nation its definite characteristics, traditions, and rites, even though the sexual problems are universal and non-national. In every nation there exists a cultured, sophisticated minority which shares its rules of behavior and its conscious ideals with similar minorities of all other nations within the same sphere of civilization; and there exists the great mass of people following their national sexual code, their peculiar unwritten but unviolable sexual laws. Lorca felt and expressed the problems of sex such as they had been shaped and transformed by the complex conventions of his people. He felt the emotions at the root of the Spanish sexual code so deeply that in his art he magnified them until traditional values stood out with a perturbing significance.

His three rural tragedies, *Bodas de Sangre, Yerma,* and *La Casa de Bernarda Alba,* show these traditions and the problems behind them with the greatest force.

Bodas de Sangre, "Blood Wedding," has a simple pattern of love, honor, and vengeance. The only son of a widow, whose husband and first-born son were killed by the men of a neighboring family, is in love with the daugh-

ter of a widower, a rich farmer like himself. A marriage
is arranged in which the father's greed for more land and
the mother's wish to bury the memory of bloodshed and
see new life created have as much part as the son's love.
The girl, however, has long been in love with the son of
the man who had killed her betrothed's father and brother.
Neither of the young men wants to carry on the feud which
is ever present in the mind of the mother. The girl has
been fighting against her passion for years and intends to
fulfill her contract. The man she loves has even married
to escape from his forbidden desire for her. But neither
he nor the girl can bear the idea that she should deliver
herself to another; they elope on her wedding day. There
is only one thing to be done. "The hour of blood has struck
again." The mother knows that she now has lost her hope
of grandchildren and will lose her only remaining son,
but she sends him in pursuit of the couple, because the
murderer of her hope must be killed—the blood of the
son of her husband's murderer must be shed. The two men
meet, fight, and kill each other.

The outline of this triangle-and-vendetta story is familiar. But Lorca has filled it with an essentially Spanish
tragedy.

The mother is the incarnation of this tragedy. A strong
woman who enjoyed life with her husband, she has become
dominated by the fear of the extinction of her blood—
fear of death, not for herself but for the seed—and by an
anxiety to see her physical existence continued, perpetuated by her son's children. This constant fear fills her
with a sense of doom. Vengeance of her "blood" follows
from her possessive, death-haunted love: to let the enemy's
seed survive one's own would mean final death.

Centuries of Moorish and medieval-Catholic breeding,

centuries of a social order in which women were valued
only for the sons they produced, created this attitude. The
code which sprang from it is still valid in Spain. Lorca's
"mother," who likes men to be lusty and wild because it
means more sons, is deeply convinced that procreation and
fecundity are the object, not the correlate, of married sexual love. Her son must marry to give her, the mother,
grandchildren: ". . . and see to it that you make me
happy by giving me six grandchildren, or as many as you
like, since your father did not have the time to make me
more sons."

She glories in man's procreative strength: "Your grandfather left a son at every corner," she says proudly to her
son. But she believes that a man must not only beget children but also engender life around him, be fecund in every
sense.

Mother and son talk about this while they are walking
over the land of his betrothed:

> SON: These are dry lands.
> MOTHER: Your father would have covered them
>   with trees.
> SON: Without water—?
> MOTHER: He would have found it. In the three
>   years he lived with me, he planted ten cherry
>   trees, the three walnut trees by the mill, a
>   whole vineyard, and the plant called Jupiter
>   which had scarlet flowers and withered.

This moral conviction that men and women must be
fecund and that the man and husband is the master because he is the instrument of fecundation has the deepest
possible psychological and social roots. In peasant com-
munities it is kept alive in its ancient form by a powerful

economic fact: there must be sons to work the land and to defend the property. In Spain this law was reinforced by the rules of the Moorish harem, rules which influenced the non-Moorish society of the country and survived the expulsion of the Moors. It was adjusted, exalted, and perpetuated in the stern teachings of the Church, which made it sinful for husband and wife to enjoy each other, but righteous to multiply. The code of honor which demands the taking of life and the preservation of virginity, not for the sake of "virtue" or love but for the sake of the purity of the "blood," is part of this tradition; it provides the sanctions against sexual offenses and protects the property of the family.

This code and the elements that went into its making were by no means confined to Spain. But the interesting point is that the code is still real to Spaniards, including those who have rationally repudiated it. Even in the towns, the same men and women who will look unmoved at the display of an exaggerated "point of honor" in some of the plays of Calderón and Lope de Vega are stirred by the sterner, simpler justice of the *Alcalde de Zalamea*, the village mayor who kills the violator of his daughter and earns the approval of the King for his act. And they are moved in the recesses of their consciousness by the ancient popular emotions crystallized in Lorca's images.

In fact, blood feud and its code of honor are things of this age, not merely of the past, to Spaniards. The modern laws have prosecuted and suppressed vendettas, but they were powerless against family feuds which lasted through generations and destroyed generations. The same fierce possessive love and haunting fear of extinction which drive the mother in Lorca's tragedy, drove many women during the Spanish Civil War and, through children steeped in

hatred against the murderers of their "blood," threaten to
breed relentless feuds for generations to come.

On this hard soil, the code of the blood is stronger than
love. The mother in *Bodas de Sangre* admits no justification for the betrayal of the law of purity. A woman must
have no lover. Contemptuously she says of the girl who
followed her beloved: "Honest women, clean women, go
into the water. But not she." This rule is accepted by the
girl herself. She knows that she did wrong in following
the other man, whom she could never marry, and in wanting to live with him. She accepts the law that the honor of
the family and her own honor are safe only if her virginity
is left intact for her husband to convert it into maternity.
When the two dead bodies have been carried back to
the village the unfaithful bride goes to the house of her
dead bridegroom's mother and faces her curses. The
mother cries out: "But his honor—what about his honor?"
The bride then justifies her "crime," not by her love but
by the other man's fatal erotic attraction. Fiercely she
defends her "intact" honor, ready to pass through an
ordeal by fire to prove it:

> I want her to know that I am pure. That I may
> be mad, but that if they were to bury me now,
> no man would have seen himself in the white-
> ness of my breasts. . . . For I went away with
> the other one. I went. You would have done the
> same. I was a seared woman, covered with sores
> within and without, and your son was a trickle of
> water from which I hoped to get children, land,
> and health. But the other was a dark leaf-grown
> river, he overcame me with the sound of reeds,
> singing through his teeth. And I went along with

your son who was like a little child of cold water,
and the other sent me hundreds of birds which
would not let me walk and which left white frost
on my wounds, the wounds of a poor blighted
woman, of a girl kissed by fire. . . . But what
you say—no. I am clean and honest as a new-
born girl child, and I am strong enough to prove
it to you. Light the fire. We shall put our hands
in the flame. You for your son, I for my body.
And you will be the first to drop your hands.

The lyrical language is the poet's, but the images come
from the speech people of the Andalusian countryside use
in emotional moments, describing their passions and half-
comprehended thoughts in ageless, occult metaphors, as
though in magic formulas.

Bodas de Sangre ends with a lament in which the mother,
the girl, and the women of the village speak of death in
tender, sensuous words:

[11]   He was a beautiful horseman,
　　　now—a heap of snow.
　　　He stormed hills and fairs
　　　and women's arms.
　　　Now dusky moss
　　　crowns his brow.

　　　Sunflower of your mother,
　　　mirror of the earth,
　　　let them put on your breast
　　　a cross of bitter oleander,
　　　let a sheet cover you,
　　　of gleaming silk,

let water pour its grief
between your still hands.

Oh, the four young men
come back with weary shoulders!

Oh, the four gallants
bear with them death.

Neighbors—
                they are bringing them!

It does not matter.
The Cross—the Cross—

sweet nails,
sweet Cross,
sweet name
of Jesus.

May the Cross shelter the quick and the dead!

Neighbors, with a knife,
with a little knife,
on an ordained day, between two and three,
two men killed each other for love.
With a knife,
with a little knife
that scarcely fills the hand,
but its fine point pierces
the startled flesh
and stops in the place
where entangled quivers
the dark root of the cry.

And this is a knife,
a little knife
that scarcely fills the hand—
fish without scales or river—
that on an ordained day, between two and three,
two men may lie stiff
with waxen lips.

And it scarcely fills the hand,
but its fine point pierces
the startled flesh
and stops there, in the place
where entangled quivers
the dark root of the cry.

In reshaping the old, familiar, half-forgotten tale Lorca
thus made visible not merely the behavior of people possessed by their blood code, but the "dark root of the cry"
in a ritual in which sex is possession of life and salvation
from death, but death the final, ordained frustration. To
this ritual all Spaniards respond.

But *Bodas de Sangre* was translated into French and
English and staged in Paris, London, and New York. I was
in Paris in 1938 when the play was a failure with the
public, despite an excellent translation and in spite of
praise from critics who mixed admiration for fighting
Republican Spain with a mystical—and snobbish—admiration for the "blood and soil" quality and the lyrical
symbolism of Lorca's text. It was bound to fail, because
foreign spectators understood it only through a labored
intellectual process, not through the swift, piercing associations and sensations it produced in a Spanish public.
Indeed, in any Spanish-speaking public—for in Hispano-

America it was a success as profound and lasting as in
Spain itself. In his introduction to the translations of Lorca
poems, which I quoted before, R. M. Nadal speaks of the
failure of the play in New York and then says: "Whether
we like it or not, Spain is from many points of view a
world apart, and an attempt to transfer, in Lorca's most
Spanish poetry, Spanish values of men and things meets
with an almost unsurmountable barrier."

I am even more conscious of this barrier in speaking
of Lorca's second rural tragedy, *Yerma*, although the
essence of its theme is truly human in the most universal
sense of the word.

The very title is untranslatable. *Yermo* is an adjective
which means uncultivated, unsown, untilled, barren, waste,
as in *tierras yermas*, waste lands. Here *la yerma*, "the
barren one," means a woman who is sterile not through
a physical defect but because she has never been made
fecund—because she was denied the seed. *La Yerma* of
the play is utterly convinced that motherhood is withheld
from her because her husband, by no means physiologi-
cally impotent and living in a so-called normal relationship with her, does not "put his will to having children,"
but only wants to possess and enjoy her body.

La Yerma married because she wanted to have children
from her man. She never felt, and never wished to feel,
any pleasure in the sexual act. So she explains herself to an
old neighbor woman who asks her:

> "Listen—does your husband please you?"
> "What do you mean?"
> "Do you want him? Do you long to be with
> him . . . ?"
> "I don't know."

"Don't you tremble when he comes near you? Don't you feel as in a dream when he puts his lips to yours? Tell me."

"No. I never felt like that."

"Never? Not even when you were dancing?"

"Maybe—once—Victor. . . . He took me round my waist and I couldn't say anything because I couldn't speak. . . . But it was only because I was ashamed. . . . It's different with my husband. My father gave him to me and I accepted him. With joy—that is the simple truth. The first day I was betrothed to him I thought already of the children. And I looked at myself in the mirror of his eyes. Yes, but all I saw there was myself, very small, very docile, as if I were my own daughter."

"Just the opposite of me. Perhaps this is why you haven't borne children yet. Girl, the men must give us pleasure. They must undo our plaits and let us drink water from their mouth. That's what keeps the world going round."

"Your world, not mine. I think many things, very many, and I'm certain that my son will make the things I think come true. It is for his sake that I gave myself to my husband and I go on giving myself to him so that my son should come, but never for pleasure."

"And so you're empty."

"No, not empty, because I'm getting full of hate. Tell me—is it my fault? Is it necessary to seek the man in the man and nothing else? But then, what is there to think of when he leaves you on the bed, sadly staring at the ceiling, while he

turns his back on you and falls asleep? Need I
go on thinking of him, or of that which may
spring from my body, shining with light? . . ."

Yerma's obsession is not only an individual problem,
it is the tragic outcome of an upbringing which twists,
coarsens or starves the spontaneous feelings of young
women. Lorca shows this, indirectly but none the less with
an almost cruel clarity, through the way in which he lets
the women talk about themselves. Yerma complains: "Girls
like me who grow up in the country find all doors closed.
Everything is turned into half-spoken words and gestures,
because they say that one mustn't know about such things."
"Such things" are matters of sex and love. The old woman
to whom Yerma appeals refuses to talk to her as she would
to a "more balanced" person, but she counters Yerma's
"May God protect me!" with an oblique explanation:
"God? No. I've never liked him. When will you realize
that he doesn't exist? It's the men who have to help
you. . . . But it is true, there ought to be a God, at least
a little one, and he ought to send his lightnings down on
the men of a rotten seed who turn all the gaiety of the
fields into stagnant water."

Yerma does not know what she means. She insists on
telling herself and others: "A woman of the land who
produces no children is as useless as a bunch of thorns,
and bad, too, even if I myself belong to that rubbish cast
away by the hand of God." In accepting this doctrine she
blocks every way to escape and withdraws even further into
herself. As she cannot admit any fault of her own and cannot see that she has come near to killing an essential part of
her inner self, she can only turn against the instrument
that fails her, her husband.

She never ceases to brood over her wrongs. Because the child does not come though she knows her body is ready for it, she feels defeated and hurt in her unfulfilled motherhood. While she is externally obedient she is accumulating an obscure hatred of the husband who takes his pleasure with her—a pleasure she cannot and will not share. She convinces herself that he refuses her the spiritual cooperation in creating a child and so imposes barrenness on her. There is the other man, Victor, who has the power to stir her senses and would, so she believes, give her the child. But her rigid code forbids her to acknowledge this solution; she cannot take him as a lover, she cannot leave her husband and live with Victor. Thus she goes on guarding her husband's and her own "honor," half proud, half despairing of her frigidity in his arms. She tries witchcraft, but it does not help. Her torturing physical hunger for the child—the only life she can feel—shakes her with brainstorms. She whips herself into ecstasy:

[12]   Oh, what meadow of pain,
        oh, what door shut to beauty!
        I want to suffer for a child, and the wind
        offers me dahlias like slumbering moons.
        These two wellsprings I have in me
        of warm milk, they are in the tautness
        of my flesh two horse-strong pulses
        shaking the branch of my anguish.
        Oh, blind breasts under my gown,
        oh, eyeless, sheenless doves!
        Oh, how my imprisoned blood aches
        and pricks my neck with wasp stings!
        But you will come, love, my child,
        for the water bears salt, the earth fruit,

and our wombs guard soft little children
as the cloud carries sweet rain.

Happier or less sensitive women glory in their physical
love for their husbands, proud to bear their children, or
they accept things as they come with all the gaiety they
can muster. They have no patience with Yerma; one of
them says: "A woman who wants children gets them." If
they pity Yerma, it is because they dislike her dour husband, particularly since he has brought his unmarried,
bigoted sisters into his house to keep watch on his wife.
To the robust village women those spinsters appear "like
those huge leaves which sometimes grow on graves—
they're coated with candle wax." But despite this partisan-
ship, their gossip and the songs they sing while washing
their linen down by the river have a scarcely hidden sting
for the childless wife:

[13]   I wash your ribbon
        in the cold stream.
        Your laughter is like
        warm jessamine.
        I want to live in
        the little snow shower
        of the jessamine.

        Oh pity the dried-up wife,
        her whose breasts fill with sand!

        Tell me if your husband
        gives you seed,
        that the water may sing
        in your shift.
        . . . .

My husband comes
from the hills for his meal.
He gives me a rose
and I give him three.

My husband is home
from the plain for supper.
The live coal he gives me
I cover with myrtle.
. . . .
It's groaning in the sheets—
and it's singing a song—
when the man brings us
the bread and the crown.

For the arms entwine—
and light in our throat overspills—
and the stem of the twigs grows sweet—
and the tents of the wind hide the hill.

So that a child may melt
the cold glaze of dawn. . . .

Yerma feels an outcast from the teeming life around
her:

I am hurt, utterly hurt and humbled when
I see the young shoots of the wheat, and that
the springs never cease pouring water, and that
the sheep bear hundreds of lambs—and the
bitches . . . and it is as if the fields were rising
to show me their young broods in their slumber,
while I feel two hammers beating me here [she
beats her breasts] instead of the mouth of my
own child.

While Yerma turns herself into a possessed priestess of
maternity, her quarrels with her husband become increas-
ingly bitter and devoid of tenderness, of mutual understanding. In the end Yerma runs away from her arid home
on a crazy pilgrimage to a little sanctuary in the mountains which is popularly supposed to cure sterile women.
To some of the pilgrims it is a religious act; to many more
the pilgrimage is a chance "to meet new men—and then
the Saint works the miracle," in the cynical words of the
old woman. Prayers and folk songs mix with pagan fer-
tility rites:

[14]   Lord, that the rose may flower,
            leave me not in the shadow.

            Let the yellow rose
            flower on her wilted flesh,
            and in the womb of thy servants
            the dark flame of the earth. . . .

            "Let her say for whom she hopes,
            let her say for whom she waits,
            ay, with her dry womb
            and her color pale."

            "When the night comes I'll say it,
            when the bright night comes.
            In the night of the pilgrimage
            I shall rip my petticoat's flounce." . . .

            When you go on the pilgrimage
            to pray that your womb may open,
            do not wear the veil of mourning,

but a soft shirt of cambric.
Come alone, behind the walls
where the closed fig trees stand,
and bear my earthen body
till the white moan of dawn. . . .

Now hit her with the horn—
with the rose and the dance—
ah, how the married wife sways! . . .

Heaven has gardens
with rose trees of joy,
and between the rose trees,
the wonder rose!

But Yerma is withered, not in her flesh but in her soul.
The "flowering" of her body is impossible. Neither witchcraft nor religious fervor, nor the way of the world, as
the shrewd old woman suggests it, can free her from her
frustration. Everything wells up in her when she meets for
the last time her husband, who has come after her. When
he wants to persuade her to be happy with him without
thought of a child, she cries out:

"What was it you sought in me?"
"You."
"Oh, yes. You sought a home, quiet, a woman.
But nothing more. Is it true what I am saying?"
"It is true. I, and everybody else."
"But the other things? And your son?"

Fully realizing the hopelessness of her quest, afraid of
bringing "dishonor" on her husband, she chokes life out of
him with the desperate strength of madness. By his dead
body she tells the gathered crowd:

Withered, withered. But safe. Now I know for
certain. Alone. I shall rest without waking with
a sudden start to see whether my blood tells me
of the coming of another, of new blood. My body
dried up forever. What do you want to know?—
Don't come near me, for I have killed my child.
I myself, I have killed my child.

I imagine that this tragedy strikes the majority of non-
Spaniards as the lyrical exaltation of a clinical case, mov-
ing only in its poetic force, but strange and unreal. To a
Spanish public it is a soul-shaking experience.

Here is a cry from the tortured soul of a Spanish woman
encased in the armor of implacable laws, half Christian
and half pagan. In the everyday reality of Spanish life
those laws—"You shall bear children in pain" and "You
must obey your husband who is your owner and master"—
have become mitigated and blurred by compromise, un-
dermined by the slow evolution of a new moral code. A
woman such as Yerma cannot achieve a compromise. In
her, a single commandment—the woman must marry, not
for love but to bear children—has cast out all the others,
so that her eroticism is bound up with her dream child,
and the concrete relationship with her husband is reduced
to the barest sexual intercourse for the sake of conception.
It is Lorca's supreme art that through this exceptional case,
not intended to be "realistically" sound, the Spanish public conceives the full meaning of a code the ultimate conse-
quences of which are usually ignored because it is no longer
obtrusive enough to be discovered in the innumerable small
frustrations and spiritual distortions of sexual life. To this
public Yerma's actions are, within her code, inevitable and
right. But the nakedness of her emotions and the crude,

clear discussion of the sexual act, sperm and spirit, not only bare but also attack the roots of this code.

Again, the surface moral of Lorca's play is traditional and in the Spanish-Catholic sense conventional: the poet seems to accept these "Spanish values of men and things." But he sets them out against the deeper-seated "eternal laws of the heart and mind of man," to use his own words, against the irresistible life and joy in life which unite men and women. He shows the moral conventions applied with such an uncompromising completeness and self-revealing sterility that he provokes mental rebellion against them —above all against the spiritual mold of Spanish women. For both *Bodas de Sangre* and *Yerma* place the conflict in the soul of women and show the problems of sex from the women's side rather than from the men's, because the crushing load of frustration falls on them.

There is an ascending scale of frustration in the plays which Lorca wrote in the last three years of his life, and in each of them women are destroyed by their acceptance of the somber moral code of their social world. In his last play, *La Casa de Bernarda Alba*, published nine years after his death and in a version he may not have considered final, he exposed this code in its most sinister shape. He called his play "Drama of Women in the Villages of Spain," to announce its bitter general significance, and a footnote says: "The poet warns the public that these three acts are meant as a photographic documentary," thus leaving no doubt of the typical and, within these limits, realistic character of the scenes. Lorca's friend Angel del Río reports that the raw material of the tragedy was provided by "a family which really used to live near Fuentevaqueros," in the district of the poet's home; another friend,

Adolfo Salazar, recalls that Lorca, reading his play aloud,
proudly exclaimed after each scene: "Not a drop of poetry!
Reality! Realism!"

The personages of the play are all women. It is set in
the country house of Bernarda Alba, a caste-proud and
wealthy widow with five daughters, one of them rich in
her own right as the sole child and heir of the first husband. The village itself lies in a hot plain. It is far from
the river, its inhabitants drink their water from wells and
live a life as stagnant as that water. Its women, as far as
they are not in domestic service or on the verge of beggary,
live and die within the walls of their whitewashed houses.
To go to church is their main diversion. There the young
girls may see the men of the neighborhood, spied upon by
the eyes of all the older women. The men have more freedom. They are at least in the fields during the day. Even
if they break out from their domestic confines and find
their pleasure with the one "bad woman" of the village,
or with a married woman, or with a stranger from the outside world, they are forgiven because they are men. But
their women pay for it. None of the families of the village
are accepted as equals by Bernarda Alba, who sits in the
house she inherited from her father as in a castle. Even
during the lifetime of her easygoing second husband she
had imposed her steely will on her household. After his
death—this is the starting point of the play—she enjoys
her sole possession of power and property, determined not
to let it be frittered away by the marriage of her daughters,
except that of the eldest, the heiress in her own right.
Bernarda condemns the girls to nunlike seclusion during
the traditional eight years of mourning for their father:
"For the eight years of the mourning not even the wind of
the street may enter this house. We must think of the win-

dows and doors as being blocked up with bricks. So it was
done in my father's and my grandfather's house. During
the time, you can begin with the embroidery for your
dowry."

But the four know only too well that there is little chance
of their getting husbands. Their shares in the estate are
small, not tempting for suitors, and no man can even come
to see them now. It is particularly bitter for all of them
that Angustias, the wealthy stepsister, should be betrothed
to the handsome Pepe Romano, the only man of the social
class whom they used to see. It is hardest for young Adela,
who is passionately in love with him and knows that he
has desired her, even though he is willing to marry the
money and lands of her ugly, aged sister. Adela is proud
of her young body, afraid of withering away behind the
bleak, whitewashed walls of the house, and willing to fight
for her right to love. Every night, after Pepe Romano has
paid a dutiful call to his betrothed, Angustias (a call which
consists in the traditional conversation through the wrought-
iron grille of her window), he lingers on outside Adela's
window rails until the small hours of the morning—and
their encounter is passionate. Adela can hide her love and
desperate determination from her mother, but not from
her sister Martirio. Martirio is the second youngest, a
hunchback with an ardent body, racked by suppressed desire. Once, only once, a man had wanted to court her, but
because his father used to be a common laborer, Bernarda
had driven him off. Martirio had been waiting for him in
vain behind her barred window, with nothing but a night-
dress to clothe her deformity and her desire. Then she had
been kindled by the sight of Pepe Romano, and his daily
visit to the windows of her sisters is now driving her
crazy. Hiding her hatred and longing under a meek sub-

mission, she spies on Adela. She might resign herself to
the conventional marriage between the man and Angustias,
because there would never be any joy and love in it, but
she cannot bear the thought that Adela should have what
would always be denied to herself. Of the remaining two
sisters, one, Amelia, is spared suffering by her almost infantile, brainless vacuity, while the other, Magdalena,
saves her sanity by desperate cynicism and a clear-sighted
resignation to her fate. Neither of them can do anything
to halt the currents of passion released by the invisible
presence of the male.

These currents are clearly seen by an old family re-
tainer, half beggarwoman, half servant, who is the only
person to speak openly to Bernarda. Old Poncia brings a
breath of vulgar gaiety and shrewdness into the cloistered
house; she speaks to the girls of the normal, brutal, gusty
life shared by men and women outside. But even this
sturdy, warm-blooded woman has been warped by her
thirty years' bondage in Bernarda's house; she has turned
sly and malicious, resentful of the arrogant contempt with
which she is treated. For Bernarda's pride of caste kills
every human approach. Though she likes hearing village
gossip from Poncia, she grants her no right of companion-
ship. "Poor folk are like beasts, they seem to be made
from another stuff than we." Poncia rebels against Bernarda's rule, but she half accepts her rules. She would like
to prevent a catastrophe which she sees coming when Angustias' impending wedding drives Adela to a reckless
decision, but has not the courage and selflessness to act.
The only soul in the house who is beyond the reach of
Bernarda's soulless code is her old mother—who is a mad-
woman. She escapes from her room and tells her crazy
truth: "I want fields. I want houses, but open houses where

the women lie in bed with their little children and the men
sit in the open on their chairs. Pepe Romano is a giant.
All of you want him. But he will devour you because you
are nothing but grains of corn. No, not grains of corn.
You are frogs without tongues." Her lunacy reveals the
suppressed madness in these women's unnatural life, but
it does not help the other prisoners of Bernarda's house.

In a sultry summer night, when the stallion of the farm-
yard drums with his hooves on the stable door until he is
let out, Adela commits her final act of revolt. She meets
her sister's betrothed out in the open. When Martirio sur-
prises her on her return to the house, she cries out that she
will never again stay in their "prison." She will brave the
opinion of their world—the world of the village which
hounds rebels to death—and she will live in freedom where
her lover will be able to see her at his pleasure, after his
barren marriage with her sister. Martirio is mad with rage
and envy of Adela's "triumphant body." She rouses Bernarda and denounces Adela: "She's been with him! Look,
her petticoat is covered with straw." The impassioned girl
tells the whole house that she is his "wife" and that he is
outside in the garden, "strong as a lion." Bernarda takes
a rifle and goes on the chase, followed by Martirio. The
other women hear a shot; Martirio comes back to tell them
that Pepe Romano is finished. This is a lie. Bernarda has
missed him, he has escaped on his horse. But Adela does
not stay to hear this. Her lover has been killed: she goes
and hangs herself. And now Bernarda's stony conviction of
the rightness of her code is stronger than any feeling. She
orders her daughters to lay out Adela in her room, in a
virgin's shroud. For this is to be the truth and the story
which the world will hear: "We shall bury ourselves in a
sea of mourning. She, the youngest daughter of Bernarda

Alba, has died a virgin. Have you heard me? Silence, I tell
you, silence. Silence!" The honor of the house of Bernarda
Alba is saved. Nothing else matters. Death is stronger than
rebellious life.

In black on white—the black of sterile mourning set
against the dead white of a prisonhouse—Lorca's play
shows the working of the old Spanish code of honor and
caste in its deadly extremes, valid and fatal in a sector of
society where there is no outlet, no hope of sanity and
freedom, for the hysteria of frustrated women. Erotic
frustration and perverted power are certainly not specifically Spanish; but their tragic fatality that seems so inevitable to its victims is a characteristic element of the
Spanish world from which Lorca took his characters and
his plot. It was the "black" Spain which killed Lorca himself, two months after the day—June 19, 1936—when he
finished the "Drama of Women in the Villages of Spain."

The exceptional sensitiveness to feminine reactions
which fills Lorca's plays runs through the whole of his
poetry, wherever it touches themes of love, and even when
the man appears as the actor and conqueror. Perhaps it
was this power to identify himself with both men and
women which made it possible for Lorca to capture and
express all the main elements in Spanish sexual consciousness, including those subtly entangled with the religious
life of the people.

Spanish children first learn about the supreme value of
chastity in men and virginity in women through the stories
of saints and martyrs on which religious tuition centers
during the early years of childhood. Except for St. Anna,
the mother of the Virgin—of the "Immaculate Conception"
—most of the female saints in Spanish hagiology and

martyrology are virgins. In popular language "virgin" and "martyr" are always coupled. Through their religious instruction and their studies of classical literature Spanish boys are forced to visualize the female body as a "sack of uncleanliness" and to imagine its putrefaction in slow, loathsome stages. They are shown the virginal martyrs in the clean loveliness of their young flesh and in the horror of their mutilated bodies. Perversely, a deeper exaltation and a deeper compassion are produced when the breasts hacked off by the executioner are described as young and virginal than when they are the good tired breasts of a mother of many children. Young boys and girls are taught to long for a martyr's death which, in the midst of unbearable pain, contains the searing joy of union with the Savior, the felicity of a transition to a better life. This educational process breeds, particularly in the girls, the ideas and ideals of Lust through Pain, Holiness through Horror, and Virginity triumphant over Violence and crowned by the Heavenly Bridegroom. Juvenile sado-masochism is cultivated by those unimpeachable legends and developed by the terrifying, grimly naturalistic paintings of martyred saints in Spanish churches, where the air is thick with sensuous exaltation, cruel and cloying.

This atmosphere, as powerful and all-pervading as the Catholic Church of Spain itself, cannot fail to have a deep, though varied, effect on the minds of young people. Very often it produces a precocious awareness of sex, combined with fear. Children search for an explanation of words and values which from their seventh year onward they are told to memorize, accept, and even discuss in the Confessional, when the Father Confessor asks them: "Have you fornicated?" Often it breeds an early mysticism. Immunized to the outer world by the ecstasies of carnal visions hallowed

by a religious appearance, those young mystics are convinced that the other sex is an instrument of evil and that
chastity is the same as sanctity. Girls steeped in this conviction frequently degenerate to pathetic and dangerous
old spinsters of the type known as *beatas*, who, single-
minded and infantile, haunt Spanish churches and homes.
And the same atmosphere helps to breed an astonishingly
great number of sexual introverts, extroverts, and perverts,
of sadists and masochists, and an even greater number of
people who come near to being one or the other.

Lorca touched upon all those undercurrents of emotion
and behavior, laying bare the strange basic forces in that
which seemed orthodox and impeccable. So is his ballad
"The Martyrdom of St. Eulalia" not so much imbued with
mystic exaltation as with sexual cruelty:

[15]   . . . The Consul demands a salver
              for Eulalia's breasts.
              A bundle of green veins
              bursts from her throat.
              Her sex trembles, a bird
              entangled in thorns.
              Her severed hands roll
              on the ground, unguided
              and yet still crossing
              in faint, beheaded prayer.
              Through the red holes
              where her breasts had been
              show diminute heavens
              and rivulets of white milk.
              Thousand saplings of blood
              cover her back
              and oppose humid trunks

> to the lancet of the flames. . . .
> The Consul carries on a salver
> Eulalia's smoke-singed breasts.

This description, most unbearably cruel where the images are most gentle, lifts the mantle of pious convention from a vision burned deep into the minds of Spanish schoolboys. But in its poetical form it continues the tradition of classical sacred poetry.

The beautiful novel *El Obispo Leproso,* by Gabriel Miró—who was so deeply religious that his hatred for certain aspects of Spanish clerical education was overwhelming—has a chapter on that interplay of adolescent eroticism and martyrology:

Young Pablo is contemplating the pictures of female saints in a pious book. He does not look at the male saints. But he caresses the naked foot of one holy nun with the tip of his finger, longs to kiss the flaming red lips of another, and thinks of a living woman when he sees the ripe bosom of a third. His teacher, the Jesuit P. Bellod, catches him out and punishes him by reading to him the description of a particular kind of torture, which leaves the martyr rotting in the sun until he "feels his flesh seething, molten to a paste." He tells the boy that the book also contains "the outrages and tortures suffered by many Christian virgins, which you must not see in any circumstances." This has the obvious results:

> "And the next evening, he searched for the forbidden illustrations. He held himself in check, looking at his fingers as they trembled like P. Bellod's. He saw women saints impaled, quartered, broken on the wheel, crushed by the ham-

mer. When he came to the ordeal of the virgin
Engratia, he read greedily the verse by Pruden-
tius:

[16]   You alone vanquish death.
            You live, the deep hole
            In your rent flesh pulsating.
            An unclean hand
            lacerated your flesh.
            As the breasts were cut,
            your heart showed naked.
            Gangrene gnawed your marrow
            and sharp hooks tore
            your entrails to tatters."

All this was Lorca's raw material—and he made its
"heart show naked."
There is another important side to religious eroticism
as it exists in Spain today. The terrible realism of the
old, stern images of Christ on the Cross and of tortured
saints was followed in Renaissance and Baroque art by
the sensuous idealization of beauty in the paintings or
sculptures of beings "in the Glory," the Virgin, the beati-
fied saints, the archangels—including the fallen Lucifer—
and the hosts of the angels. The sinless, disembodied subjects gave the artists liberty to create stainless, "immaculate" bodies, and justified, indeed demanded, adoring contemplation. It is impossible not to feel the bodily warmth
of Murillo's glowing, oversweet Virgins and female saints.
Less obvious, but of greater psychological importance, is
the physical fascination of the images of juvenile male
martyrs—such as St. Sebastian—and above all of the
angels. In them women who had been taught to renounce

all sensual thoughts of the masculine body found "innocent," concrete shapes on which their imagination was allowed to dwell. The traditional images of the archangels are androgynous, and the Baroque artists particularly created ideal forms of an ambiguous beauty which is not sexless, but belongs to neither sex, and to both. In Murcia there is a polychrome wood sculpture of the archangel Gabriel, by the eighteenth-century monk Salzillo, in which feminine and masculine elements are inextricably fused to a gentle, perfect, and seductive shape of great purity. Precisely this image is the dream love of one of the women in Gabriel Miró's novel; it helps her to keep her emotional life untouched by the somber, greedy masculinity of her bigoted husband and renders her helpless when she meets the candid, loving desire of a beautiful adolescent boy.

On a lower level, this inhibited eroticism finds an outlet in the sugary sweetness with which pious Spanish women love to clothe their favorite male saints and angels. In Lorca's *Romancero Gitano* there is the poem of St. Michael, archangel-patron of Granada:

[17]   In the alcove of his tower
Saint Michael, covered with lace,
shows his beautiful thighs
wreathed with ruffles.

The Archangel, domesticated
in a twelfth-hour gesture,
feigns a gentle fury
of nightingales and feathers.
Saint Michael sings at the windows,
ephebe of three thousand nights,
fragrant of eau-de-cologne

and very far from the flowers.
. . . .
Saint Michael stayed still
in the alcove of his tower,
his petticoats stiff
with insets and sequins.

It sounds like a satire, but it is merely a cruelly clear
visualization. In every one of the thousands of Spanish
churches the holy images are in the care of the *beatas*. It
is only too patent why those withered spinsters and stern
matrons and timid, intense girls clothe masculine saints—
or androgynous but traditionally manly archangels—in
feminine apparel. These saints parade in women's shifts
under their draperies, or in starched petticoats stiff with
embroidery over tinseled drawers with lace edgings—the
"ruffles" of the poem. With the images of the archangels
the women's phantasy has free play. Strong St. Michael
and the sweetly feminine St. Raphael of tradition are be-
dizened with multicolored silk ribbons, particularly in
Andalusia and more particularly in cities like Granada,
Lorca's own town.

This fashion of decorating images is by no means limited to saints and angels, who after all rouse esthetic
feelings and appeal to the sense of beauty. The same taw-
dry foppery appears in the dress of the most tragic images;
not even the Crucified Christ escapes it. In his book *The
Soul of Spain* (Constable, 1908), Havelock Ellis gives the
following description:

> I recall, for instance, a most sorrowful Christ
> which I came across not long since over an altar
> in an aisle of Palencia Cathedral. It was a large

wooden image on a crucifix, carved in the Spanish realistic muscular style, and around the waist
there was a charming little embroidered skirt,
very short, and below it peeped out a delicate
lace petticoat, a coquettish disguise made to sug-
gest and not to conceal, for there was nothing to
conceal. Such is the piquant figure that Spanish
religion devises for the adoration of Spanish
women, and the bent dolorous face looks more
dolorous than ever with eyes turned to this ballet-
girl's costume.

Lorca's clear vision of this religious display could draw
on the memories of his childhood when he arranged religious processions and miracle plays for children of his
own age. He must have delighted in the colors and fantastic trimmings, the masques and monumental altars of
Granada's traditional Holy Week as it was before shows
for tourists destroyed its moving poetry and unorthodox
sense of myth. He spoke of this in a broadcast in 1936:

At that time it was a Holy Week as of lace, of
canaries fluttering between the candles of the
show altars, with an air so tepid and melancholy
as though it had been asleep, the whole day long,
on the opulent bosoms of the spinsters of Granada who walk about on Maundy Thursday
yearning for the officer, the judge, the professor
from outside who would take them away. The
city was like a slow merry-go-round, swinging
in and out of the churches which were of an
astounding beauty, a fantasy of the caverns of
death and at the same time of theatrical apothe-
osis. . . . In one of the houses of the street

where coffins and wreaths for poor people are on
sale the "Roman Soldiers" met for their rehears-
als. They were not members of a Confraternity
. . . but hired men: street porters, bootblacks,
and people just out of hospital after an illness
who needed to earn a *duro*.

Thus delicate beauty and sumptuous show, the vague
desires of convention-bound women and the concrete needs
of poor workers, had impressed themselves on Lorca's sensitive mind through his early experiences of popular
Church festivals. His art lifted each of the elements to
which he had responded to its precise imaginative plane.

An early poem, *La Soltera en Misa*, "Spinster at Mass,"
describes one of those "spinsters of Granada with opulent
bosoms"—a ripe, lonely woman dressed in thick black
silk, who loses herself in the incense fumes where sex and
religious ritual merge:

[18]   Under the Moses of the incense
         you were drowsy.

         The eyes of the bull watched you.
         Your rosary trickled.

         In this gown of deep silk,
         Virginia, move not.

         Give the black melons of your breasts
         to the murmur of the Mass.

With an equal power of identification Lorca evoked the
religious world of the gypsies and the way in which they
wove sacred myths into their ingenuously carnal day-

dreams. He used their figures of speech in the gypsy
"Annunciation" of his ballad of St. Gabriel, patron of
Seville and "great-grandson" of the Giralda, Seville's
slender Moorish tower:

[19]   A beautiful lissom boy,
            wide shoulders, slim waist,
            skin of a night-pale apple,
            sad mouth and large eyes,
            sinew of fired silver,
            walks the deserted street.
            His patent-leather shoes
            bruise the dahlias of the air.
            · · · ·
            When he bends his head
            on his jasper breast,
            the night seeks for a plain,
            wanting to kneel.
            · · · ·
            Saint Gabriel, the child cries
            in the mother's womb.
            Remember that the gypsies
            gave you your suit.

On this evocation and incantation follows the white
magic of St. Gabriel's visit to the pregnant gypsy:

            Anunciación de los Reyes,
            well favored, ill dressed,
            opened the door to the star
            that came down the lane.
            Saint Gabriel, Archangel,
            between a smile and a lily,
            great-grandson of the Giralda,

was coming on a visit.
Hidden crickets chirped
in his embroidered vest,
all the stars of the night
became tinkling bells.
"Saint Gabriel, see me here,
in my heart three nails of joy.
Your radiance strews jessamine
on my glowing face."
. . . .
"God guard you, Anunciación,
well favored, ill dressed,
your son shall have three wounds
and one mole on his chest."
"Oh, Saint Gabriel, you who shine,
darling Gabriel of my life,
in the depths of my breasts
the warm milk stirs."
"God guard you, Anunciación,
mother of hundred dynasties.
Your eyes gleam arid,
landscapes for riders."

Andalusia has many convents with cool, white, shadowy
cells where women are slowly consumed by the heat of
their mystic dreams or impossible longings, until they
turn into figurines of translucent wax. They spend their
days in confectionery kitchens, mixing sugar, honey, eggs,
and almonds for the famous sweets which have names like
"Nun's Sigh," "St. Leander's Yolk," "Saint's Bones," or
"Heaven's Bacon." Or they bend over embroidery frames,
sitting among the sweet-scented flowers and herbs of a
walled garden, stitching ardent colors in fanciful patterns

for vestments or for the dowry of "their" Child Jesus. Or
they talk in the parlor with one of the old ladies who
choose to live as lodgers in a convent, because they are
tired of their relatives or frightened of the world or afraid
of a lonely death.

Such is the narrow world which Lorca conjures up in
his "Ballad of the Gypsy Nun," with its potpourri perfume
of flowers, whitewash, and spun sugar, and the distant
growl of the church organ:

[20]   Silence of whitewash and myrtle.
         Mallows in the fine grass.
         The nun stitches gilliflowers
         on straw-colored cloth.
         Seven birds of the rainbow flutter
         in the dim chandelier.
         Far off the church rumbles
         like a lazy bear.
         She embroiders so well, so deftly!
         On the straw-colored cloth
         she would love to embroider
         flowers of her fancy.
         · · · ·
         In the kitchen near by
         five citrons are candied,
         the five wounds of Christ,
         cut in Almeria.
         Two horsemen gallop
         before the nun's eyes.
         A last, faintest sound
         ruffles her shirt.
         She looks at the distant
         motionless hills and clouds

and her heart is bursting
of sugar and verbena.
Oh, what plains steeply rising,
under twenty suns,
what rivers walking as men
glimmer in her fancy!
But she goes on with her flowers. . . .

Though Lorca's poems with a religious theme or background are all similarly colored with the vision of his own Spanish region, Andalusia—far away from the Castilian monasteries with their huge stone walls and damp, dark cloisters—they provoke a sharper anticlerical reaction in a good many Spaniards than any pamphlet. They have a rebellious force because they reveal the distorted, occult, erotic element under the conventional religious cover, which all Spaniards feel, consciously or unconsciously: Lorca's poems force his public into consciousness.

Yet there runs a pagan streak through Spanish eroticism even if, in the traditional moral code guarded by the Church, it is banned from married life and altogether from the life of the women. It emerges in the man's delight in the body of a woman or another man. It breaks loose, unexpectedly, in the almost orgiastic mass festivals which transform ecclesiastic holidays or pilgrimages, such as that which Lorca brought into his story of Yerma. It is strong and joyful in some of the folk songs and folk sayings, diluted in sensuous romantic poetry, and perverted to "adulterous" passion in conventional drama. But it exists, a dark and powerful undertow, and Lorca had to give it form, just as he uncovered the other currents in the sex life of his people. And what he shows is not so much the joyous freedom or the physical delight, but rather the frightening, ruthless force of lust.

One of the best known poems in the *Romancero Gitano*, the ballad of "Preciosa and the Wind," gives to ancient Pan a shape taken from gypsy mythology. Pan bears the utterly incongruous name of the big male of Christian legend, "Saint Christopher"—*San Cristobalón*. But he is the hot, exciting wind that blows on the Andalusian seashore by night and rips all covers from desire. This wind fills Preciosa, the gypsy girl who walks in the hills beating her tambourine, with panic fear:

[21]   Preciosa comes, beating
           on her parchment moon.
           The wind who never sleeps
           saw her and rose.
           Big St. Christopher, naked,
           girdled with celestial tongues,
           looks at the girl and plays
           a sweet forlorn pipe tune:
           "Child, let me lift
           your dress to see you.
           Open to my ancient fingers
           the blue rose of your womb."

           Preciosa drops her tambourine
           and runs and does not stop.
           The big man-wind pursues her
           with a hot sword.
                . . . .
           Preciosa, run, Preciosa,
           the green wind will catch you.

Preciosa, run, Preciosa—
look where he comes,
the satyr of low stars
with shimmering tongues.

Preciosa, full of fear,
enters the house
that the Consul of the English
keeps above the pines.

. . . .

The Englishman gives the gypsy
a glass of warm milk
and a tumbler of gin
which Preciosa does not drink.

And while she tells, in tears,
her adventure to those people,
the wind, mad with rage,
bites the slates of the roof.

I recall a strange evening, when the best priest I ever
knew in my country—and one of the best men—read this
poem to us in a chilly, ugly hotel room in Madrid while
the darkness outside was torn by shell bursts. He read the
beginning (I have not quoted it), with its description of
the "amphibious path" along the shore, between crystal
water and laurel bushes, and of the dark starless silence
in which the sea laps and "sings its night full of fishes,"
while

On the peaks of the Sierra
sleep the Carabineros
who guard the white towers
where the English live.

When he came to the hot, naked wooing of the "man-wind" he stopped and exclaimed: "What a barbarian . . . 'the blue rose of your womb' . . . you see what he dares? It would make anyone afraid, it makes you feel like running away from yourself, doesn't it? But to seek cover in the white tower of English civilization—she didn't drink their lukewarm milk and gin . . ." He read on, leaving his thought unfinished.

The same frightening, ruthless intensity lives in the poem "Thamar and Amnon," in which the pagan feeling is expressed in images akin to the *Song of Songs:*

[22]   The moon turns in the sky
over waterless lands.
. . . .

Thamar was dreaming,
birds in her throat,
to the sound of cool tambourines
and moon-drenched citharas.
. . . .

Amnon, slender and intent,
watched her from the tower,
his groin filled with froth,
his beard vibrating.
. . . .

Amnon was looking
at the round and low moon
and saw in the moon his sister's
very hard breasts.
. . . .

From sealed well water
in the jars rises silence.

Stretched in the moss of tree boles
the cobra is singing.
Amnon groans on the cool,
chill sheet of his bed.
Shivers clothe with ivy
his scorched flesh.
Thamar entered silent
the silenced bedroom.

. . . .

"Thamar, in your high breasts
are two fishes that call me,
and the tips of your fingers
whisper of the cloistered rose."

. . . .

The king's hundred horses
neighed in the courtyard. . . .
Now he grips her by the hair,
now he rends her shirt.
Warm corals design
streams on a fair map. . . .

The biblical story of the violator of his sister has its
torrid landscape and desperate intensity by right of the subject. But as Lorca formed it in his verses which describe
the very act of violation in a series of images, it reaches
down to the sediments of Arab eroticism still existing in
the half-consciousness of Spanish men.

Yet all those sediments are uncovered in Lorca's most
widely popular and even hackneyed poem of love, *La
Casada Infiel*, "The Unfaithful Wife," which goes back to
the *leitmotivs* of Spanish sexual ideology: masculine honor
and virginity.

[23] And I took her to the river,
thinking she was a maid,
but she had a husband.

It was on the night of Santiago
and almost by commitment.
The street lamps went out
and the crickets lighted.
At the last corner I touched
her sleeping breasts
and they sprang open to me
like spikes of hyacinths.
Her starched petticoat
sounded in my ears
like a piece of silk
slit by ten knives.
Without silver light in their boughs
the trees grew bigger
and a horizon of dogs
barked far away from the river.
. . . .
Her thighs escaped me
like startled fishes,
half filled with fire,
half filled with frost.
That night I rode
of all roads the best,
astride a pearly mare
without stirrups or reins.
Being a man, I won't tell
the things she told me.
. . . .
I behaved as what I am,

as a true-bred gypsy.
I gave her a sewing basket,
big, of straw-colored satin,
and I refused to fall in love
because, having a husband,
she told me she was a maid
when I took her to the river.

When I read this poem to the illiterate boy from Jaen
whom Angel brought to see me in Madrid, he exclaimed:
"That's right! The bitch! Why did she want to cheat him?"

This was his first reaction. Identifying himself with
Lorca's gypsy, he did not mind so much that she was not
a virgin as that she had tried to trick him, to make him
ridiculous. It is a very common masculine reaction, but
it is particularly powerful in Spaniards, whose code of
manliness pivots on their "pride," which means their fear
of losing face. The whole poem is built on this particular
set of emotions and traditions.

It opens with the statement that the man took the woman
with him "thinking she was a maid," that is, feeling himself justified by her virginity: after all, he believed that
she was making the supreme sacrifice in his honor. Yet it
happened *casi por compromiso*, almost by commitment or
obligation, in the sense that he found himself committed
to go with her, could not escape and had to follow her
invitation. This is essential because the chase of the man
by the woman precedes the conquest of the woman by the
man. Behind the superficial Spanish Don Juan posture lies
the conviction, often expressed and more often repressed,
that up to the sexual act itself the woman has the active
role. Spanish women take this for granted, though convention demands the opposite and has imposed disguise on

the active chase. (Bernard Shaw turned it into a universal
law in *Man and Superman*.) But if the woman offers herself, the man is compelled by his honor to fulfill her wish;
otherwise he would make himself ridiculous and incur the
risk of being taken for impotent.

The gypsy in Lorca's ballad expresses freely his pride
in the conquest of a beautiful young woman, but he takes
care to show that this pride is blended with resignation at
having to accede. He praises her:

[23 cont.]
> No tuberose, no shell
> has so fine a skin,
> nor do silvered mirrors
> so glisten and gleam.

He describes his physical sensations "astride a pearly
mare," soberly indicating his own satisfying strength, but
hides in ostentatious modesty "the things she told me."
Afterward, when he takes her away "smeared with kisses
and sand," he feels the aftermath of revulsion and resent-
ment and remembers, as though in justification of this feeling, that she had caught him under false pretenses: "she
told me she was a maid, but she had a husband." He gets
rid of her by giving her a beautiful sewing basket as a
present, that is, by paying her like a prostitute. And he
feels that he has acted like the man he wants to be, "as
what I am," because, after all, could he have fallen in love
with a woman who was not a virgin but tried to trick him
into believing it?

It is hardly possible to portray the attitude of the aver-
age Spanish male more faithfully within narrow poetical
limits. All the ingredients are there:

(a) The woman tracks the man down;

(b) the man has to do his duty as a conqueror;

(c) he confers pleasure on her as an act of grace;

(d) it is not done to love a woman if she is not a virgin when she meets the man;

(e) a woman who is not a virgin may give pleasure, but she is a prostitute (except to the husband to whom she brought her virginity) and it is a rule of honor to pay her, so as to make the position clear.

I do not mean to convey that Spaniards are like this, or that their sexual relations in daily life conform to this pattern. But this is how the common Spaniard sees himself and how he feels he is, or ought to be. And here lies Lorca's immense power: He makes those obscure sediments of popular Spanish tradition visible with such an emotional impact that he clarifies them.

It may be—perhaps—a step toward clearing them away.

THE POET AND DEATH

When Federico García Lorca had been murdered, on August 19, 1936, at daybreak, in his own city of Granada, Antonio Machado wrote the lament: Machado, who in 1914 had hoped for a new youth to grow up "clear like the diamond" on the blood-drenched, rot-poisoned ground of Spain—Machado, who died in his bitter exile in 1939, surviving the younger poet by the two and a half years of the Spanish War.

He called the middle part of his lament for Lorca *El Poeta y la Muerte*, "The Poet and Death." It runs:

[24] He was seen walking with Her, alone,
unafraid of her scythe.
—First sun on tower and tower, hammers
on anvils—anvils and anvils of the forges.
Federico spoke
courting Death. And She listened.
"Because yesterday, companion, the beat
of your dry palms sounded through my verse
and you gave the ice to my song, and the edge
of your silver sickle to my tragedy,
I will sing you the flesh you have not,
the eyes which you lack,

the hair which the storm tossed,
the red lips where they kissed you. . . .
_Today as yesterday, gypsy, my Death,
how good to be with you, alone
in these winds of Granada, of my Granada!"

Two lines of this poem contain the vision of dawn in
Granada, with the first flush on her many towers and the
first sound of her day, the hammers in the countless forges
of gypsy coppersmiths. Four lines of the poem express
what all Lorca's friends knew and all his public felt: the
ever present idea of death, the intimacy with death, which
permeated and dyed his poetic work and was the over-
powering influence in his spiritual life.

The deep, impossible longing for a continuation of life,
of his life, beyond his death made him feel and live with
a haunting clarity from his beginning to his end. When he
was twenty he wrote the poem "Cicada":

[25]   Everything living that passes
          through the gates of death
          walks with lowered head
          and a white sleeping air
          · · · ·
          wrapped in the silence
          which is the cloak of death.
          · · · ·
          And may my blood in the field
          be sweet, rosy loam
          where tired laborers
          plunge their hoes.

This could have been the romantic melancholy, the
vague _Weltschmerz,_ of a very young, sensitive poet,

whether English or German or Spanish. It was something essentially different in Lorca. As soon as he outgrew the somewhat nebulous allegories and imitative forms of his very first period and found his own poetic language, consciousness of life and death emerged sharply in its full range and power, individual, Spanish, and universal.

In a poem written soon after "Cicada," in the *Balada de la Placeta,* the "Ballad of the Little Square," this consciousness has already shed the veil of vagueness. The poet listens to children playing in the "little square" and singing an old nursery song; they talk to him and he answers, nostalgically:

[26]

The children are singing
in the still night:
   "Clear stream,
     quiet spring!"

Children: What is it that keeps
your divine heart happy?

Poet: A ringing of bells
lost in the mist.

Children: Yet you leave us singing
in the little square:
   "Clear stream,
     quiet spring!"
. . . .
What is it you feel
in your red, thirsty mouth?

Poet: The taste of the bones
of my big skull.

Children: Drink the tranquil water
                of the mellow song:
                    "Clear stream,
                        quiet spring!"
                Why do you stray so far
                from our little square?
                . . . .

Poet: My silken heart
                has filled with lights,
                with the lost bells,
                and irises and bees.
                And I shall go far away,
                farther than the hills,
                farther than the sea,
                close to the stars,
                to ask Lord Jesus Christ
                that he give me back
                my heart of a child
                and my cap with the plume
                and my wooden sword. . . .

Fifteen years later, when Lorca was still young and radi-
antly successful, he wrote his *"Casida* of the Clear Death."
The early images are transfigured and darkened. He still
identifies himself with young children—I know of no other
young poet who writes of children so often and with such
a profound sadness—but he has no longer any hope of
recapturing the bright childhood world; he can only "lose
himself" in children. The awareness of the death's head
under the skin ("the bones of my big skull," as he said
in his youthful ballad) is so powerful and predominant
that it has driven out the serene nursery song:

[27]   There is no one who in giving a kiss
      does not feel the smile of the faceless people,
      no one who, touching a newborn child,
      can forget the motionless horse skulls.

      For what the roses seek in the forehead
      is a hard landscape of bones,
      and the hands of men have no other meaning
      than to copy the roots under ground.

      As I lose myself in the hearts of some children,
      I have lost myself many times in the sea.
      Ignoring the water, I go out to seek
      a death of light which would consume me.

The images of putrefaction torture him. In the "*Casida*
of the Flight" he wants to escape from them to a "clear
death":

[28]   I want to sleep the sleep of the apples,
      to be far from the tumult of the graveyards,
      I want to sleep the sleep of the boy
      who wished to cut his heart on the high seas.

      I want not again to hear that the dead lose no blood,
      that the rotted mouth continues to ask for water;
      I want not to know of the ordeal by grass
      nor of the moon with a serpent's mouth
      at work before daybreak. . . .

R. M. Nadal says that "those nearest to him knew well
how after a day of triumph, in the intimacy of conversa-

tion, he was obsessed with the idea of death and the abiding sadness of human things."

This was more than a "morbid" obsession of an oversensitive poet who never quite lost the traces of illness and the nearness of death in the first years of childhood. It was more than the individual awareness of the eternal problem of human life and death; this he shares with poets outside Spain. But outside Spain those poets were, at least after the end of the seventeenth century, an intellectual minority of artists, isolated because they were outside the stream of collective optimism. They had to oppose their visions to that glib indifference in the face of "the sadness of human things" which had become a social habit and an individual protective shell. T. S. Eliot, wrestling with "Whispers of Immortality," appealed to seventeenth-century English poets, not to a common consciousness or to familiar associations openly shared by all:

> Webster was much possessed by death
> And saw the skull beneath the skin;
> And breastless creatures under ground
> Leaned backward with a lipless grin.
>
> . . . .
>
> Donne, I suppose, was such another
> Who found no substitute for sense,
> To seize and clutch and penetrate;
> Expert beyond experience,
>
> He knew the anguish of the marrow
> The ague of the skeleton;
> No contact possible to flesh
> Allayed the fever of the bone.

In the mental climate of the world disintegrated by the
First World War, in which T. S. Eliot wrote these verses,
the bitter spiritual struggle with the "fever of the bone"
was made more bitter by its loneliness. Lorca, on the other
hand, had no need of a despairing, self-conscious irony
at his own metaphysics, because what he felt and rendered
with such relentless honesty was the death obsession of his
people. His unceasing struggle with death is ours, the
Spaniards' struggle, filtered through his creative imagination and thus made universal even in its form—and yet
purely Spanish in the realistic core of the imagery.

I do not feel equal to the task of tracing origins and
causes of the particular Spanish attitude to death. I suspect,
though, that its final mold was cast in Spain's "Golden
Age" of the Counter Reformation, when the Spanish
Church rebuilt its organization, simultaneously terrorizing
the people with the specter of death and perdition, and
promising salvation from it; then the natural acceptance
of the cycle of birth and death which belonged to medieval
Christian (and non-Christian) society was upset or destroyed. The landscape of the sierras and plains, the bareness and stagnation of social life, the "spiritual exercises"
and popular mythology all contributed to making Spain,
in Lorca's words, "a country open to death," where there
are no "blurred boundaries where men could escape into
another world."

Certainly the traditional as well as the individual Spanish reaction to the idea and reality of death is different
from that of other nations in modern Europe. Elsewhere
in European civilization, especially in England, the cer-
tainty of death is carefully shut away in a locked drawer
of the mind. The persistent uneasiness is covered up and
sublimated; everyday life is protected by a taboo on the

mention of death, which is relegated from consciousness and conversation unless it intrudes. "Eat, drink, and be merry, for tomorrow we die" puts a brisk accent on the merrymaking, not affected by the conventional warnings from the pulpits. In Spain we have been brought up to grapple with *La Intrusa*, "The Intruder," by remembering, admitting, and courting Her—as Machado's vision of Lorca puts it and as Lorca did in his art.

And Lorca was highly conscious of his share in a collective sense of life and death. He expressed it in poetry and drama. He explained it in the lectures he gave in Cuba, in 1930, when a stay in the United States had made him keenly aware of the burden of traditions, emotions, and associations which are specifically Spanish. He incorporated it in an outline of his esthetic, which he gave—in allegorical language, but with intellectual arguments underlying his lyrical prose—in a lecture on the *duende*, the dark inspiration of art which comes from the depth of the unconscious. For Lorca this daemonic inspiration ranked higher than the "muse" and the "angel," the intellectual and the spiritual forms of art with their ordered, accessible beauty. The daemonic spirit is suffering and struggle; it can reside in style or in matter, but always carries with it the suggestion of death and of new creation. Spain, because she is the "country open to death," is the country where the people acknowledge the daemonic quality in art, whether music or poetry, dance or the ritual of the bullfight. "Spain is at all times moved by the daemon." He goes on to define:

> In every country death is the end. It comes,
> and the curtains are drawn. Not in Spain. In
> Spain they are opened. There many people live

between walls until the day when they die and
are carried out into the sun. In Spain the dead
are more alive, dead, than in any other place
of the world; their profile hurts like the cutting
edge of a barber's knife. The joke about death
and the silent contemplation of death are both
familiar to Spaniards. From Quevedo's "Dream
of the Skulls" to Valdés-Leal's "Putrescent
Bishop" . . . runs a rail of saltpeter flowers.
Over this rail—versicles from Jeremiah at its
grimmest, fragrant cypress at its most lyrical—
leans a people of onlookers of death, but always
a nation where the most important things of all
have the ultimate metallic value of death.

He enumerates some of the concrete things which speak
of death to Spanish minds (and incidentally he provides
the key to many of his most obscure images):

The chopping knife, and the cartwheel, and
the clasp knife, and the prickly beard of shep-
herds, and the baldheaded moon, and the fly, and
dank cupboards, and rubble, and the images of
saints covered in lace, and quicklime, and the
stabbing outline of eaves and bay windows, they
all have in Spain the minute grasses of death,
associations and voices which an alert mind will
perceive, which recall to our memory the frozen
air of our own departure.

In another lecture which Lorca gave in Cuba he explained the sadness and the harsh realism of certain cradle
songs out of the same fundamental Spanish attitude. But
he also tried to show how this attitude is implanted in the

awakening minds of Spanish children through the cradle
songs themselves, which thus are both effect and cause:

> It is the poor women who give their children
> this melancholy fare, they who carry it to the
> houses of the rich. The child of wealthy parents
> hears the cradle song of the poor woman . . .
> those admirable servants and wet nurses who
> come down from the hills and along our rivers
> to give us the first lesson in Spanish history and
> to imprint on our flesh the stern seal of the
> Iberian motto: "Alone you are here and alone
> you shall live."

Through the popular symbols of death and the loneliness of all creatures, transformed on his poetic plane,
Lorca expressed the deepest human struggle such as it is
fought in Spanish terms, as an anonymous myth and an
individual reality.

The "gypsies" of his poems suffer from the cosmic loneliness of man. So Soledad Montoya—her name means
"solitude," as an abbreviation of "Maria of the Solitude"
—comes down from the dark hills driven by an impera-
tive longing. Her flesh is "yellow copper," it has a scent
"of horse and of shadow," but its flowering cannot assuage
the indefinable anguish of her mind:

[29]   I come to seek what I seek,
          my gaiety and my self.
               . . . .
          Do not speak to me of the sea,
          for the black sorrow sprouts
          in the lands of the olive
          under the murmur of the leaves.

There is no cure:

> Oh, sorrow of the gypsies,
> clean and ever lonely sorrow!
> Oh, sorrow of a hidden river
> and of a distant daybreak!

The gypsy Amargo—his name means "the bitter one"
—of the *Romance del Emplazado* has lost his self and
knows that he has been "summoned." In his "loneliness
without rest" he stares at a landscape of his mind, all
metal and rock, and knows as well as his neighbors that
he will have to obey the summons to death. Before the
appointed day, he learns how to face and receive his death:

[30]   Already you can, if you will,
> cut the rose-bay in your yard.
> Paint a cross on the door
> and beneath it your name,
> for hemlock and nettles
> will grow in your flank
> and the needles of quicklime
> will bite your shoes.

But the permanent consciousness of their death gives
Spaniards a profound interest in the manner, the style of
dying. The doomed man dies with dignity:

> On the twenty-fifth of June
> Amargo opened his eyes,
> and on the twenty-fifth of August
> he stretched out to close them.
> Men walked down the street
> to look at the summoned one
> who riveted to the wall

his solitude at rest.
And the unblemished sheet
in hard Roman line
gave poise to the death
with its straight folds.

Equally, the wounded smuggler chased by the Civil
Guard wishes for a decorous end:

[31]   Friend, I want to die
                  decently in my bed,
                  of steel, if it can be,
                  with sheets of fine linen.

But before this death comes, in dignity "if it can be,"
men want to snatch at any bit of color in their lives.
Lemons, those fruits which are so different on their own
soil from the shrunken, acid, meanly colored things people
of the north may buy at their grocer's, are one of the
popular Spanish symbols of life, beauty, and happiness.
The lemon tree—*limonero de mi corazón*—turns up in
innumerable folk songs and sentimental *chansons*. In his
Poema del Cante Jondo, a cycle of poems written to transmit both rhythm and spirit of those ancient "deep songs"
of the West Andalusian gypsies, Lorca puts the symbol
of a joyous life next to the symbol of drab death. It is
death such as the poor people of the southern villages
know it—the body on the floor, wrapped in a blanket, an
oil lamp beside it, and the mourners ranged along the wall:

[32]   Yellow little lemon,
                  lemon tree.
                  Throw the little lemons
                  to the wind.

Well you know it: later—
later—
an oil lamp and a blanket
on the ground. . . .

But death has to be challenged. You cannot challenge
the gray, inevitable, anonymous death which overtakes
you, though you may face it with strength and die well.
But what you can do is challenge a death you select for
yourself. A Spaniard will risk his life when it is worth
his while to die before his appointed time: then he will
think that he has mocked death and defeated it, by dying
in a manner which honors him and thus gives sense to his
losing his life.

One of the best Spanish toreros, a gypsy himself—in
the Andalusian gypsies some Spanish qualities have become so emphasized that they are quintessentially Spanish,
which may be one of the reasons why Lorca transferred
so many of his visions to the gypsy world with its naked
emotions—refused to fight a bull if he was not *bravo*, not
fierce and courageous. He said simply: "If this bull, who's
only a bullock, kills me—what then? No hard work and
no glory." Every time he faced a savage bull he would
achieve feats of incredible bravery. But if his friends then
told him: "You've risked your life," he would answer:
"It was worth while," with an undertone of uneasiness because the bull had not caught him, as though an ultimate
test had been lacking. For if the public had been forced
to recognize that only his defiance of death had led to his
goring by the bull, he would have had the right to be very
proud.

All the same, the challenge to death must not be reckless

and devoid of form, least in the bullring. Lorca says of the
art of bullfighting in his lecture on the *duende:*

> . . . it means to fight, on the one hand, with
> death which may destroy everything, and, on the
> other hand, with geometry, with the measure of
> space, the basis of the fiesta. The bull has his
> orbit, the torero has his, and between orbit and
> orbit is a point of danger which is the apex of the
> terrible game.

The code of this game with death underlies Lorca's two
ballads of the splendid gypsy youth Antoñito el Camborio
—"Antonio Torres Heredia, son and grandson of Camborios"—who goes to Seville to see a bullfight. He is happy
and in love with life:

[33]   In the middle of the journey
        he cut off round lemons
        and threw them into the water
        till it turned all golden.

But he allows himself to be ingloriously arrested by five
Civil Guards who take him to jail. It brings dishonor on
the well-bred gypsy not to throw away his beautiful life
rather than to walk along, sheepish and manacled:

> Antonio, who are you?
> If your name were Camborio,
> you would have made a fountain
> of blood with five jets.
> But you are nobody's son
> and no legitimate Camborio.

Gone are the gypsies
who once took alone to the hills!
Now the old knives lie
shivering under the dust.

Young Antonio, insulted with the worst insult, that of
being "nobody's son," redeems his honor when he fights
his four cousins, "Heredias, sons of Benamejí"—another
branch of the clan—and dies with a fine flourish. He has
deserved the ceremonious lament of his kin and the wake
of gypsy angels:

[34]   The voices of death resound
              near the Guadalquivir,
              ancient voices which ring
              the voice of a male carnation.
              He slashed their boots
              with a boar's bite.
              In the fight he made
              sleek dolphin leaps.
              He bathed his crimson tie
              in enemy blood,
              but they were four daggers
              and he had to succumb.
              . . . .
              He had three spurts of blood
              and died in profile,
              living coin that never
              will be repeated.
              A jaunty angel lays
              his head on a cushion,
              others, languidly bashful,
              have lit an oil lamp. . . .

Here the violent death was the man's deliberate choice.
But it may come unexpectedly, leaving the human being
who was alone in life more lonely when life is gone, and
dignified only through utter desolation. So one of the
"Solitude" poems in the cycle of the *Cante Jondo:*

[35]   Dead he was left in the street
            with a dagger in his breast.
            Nobody knew him.
            How the street lamp trembled,
            mother!
            How the little street lamp
            trembled!
            It was early dawn. No one
            could look at his eyes
            wide-open in the hard wind.
            And dead he was left in the street,
            a dagger in his heart,
            and nobody knew him.

For this is

[36]   Old
            earth
            of the oil lamp
            and the sorrow.
            Earth
            of the deep well shafts.

            Earth
            of the eyeless death
            and the arrows.

Every heavy, long-drawn syllable, every line consisting
of a single word, is a wail of the guitar and of a hoarse
human voice coming from some dark place of the heart:
this is how Lorca, very young still, translated the outcry
of the Andalusian people into poetry. For a long time,
until his great "Lament for the Bullfighter Ignacio Sánchez Mejías," death in its violent form predominated in
his work, as it dominated folk art. It may be that to people
who, by their traditional way of thinking, are so fiercely
jealous of their individual existence as the Spaniards, a
death by violence with its mystic smell of blood appears
less tragic and futile than a simple human end, because
it is a last arrogant assertion of will and because knife
and bullet are more concrete, more comprehensible than
the mere way of all flesh.

Yet Federico García Lorca did not respond only to the
awareness of death among his people and to its ritual
expression. He had his personal struggle with death and
with his own subjective consciousness of death. He suffered
from the Spanish philosophy which Miguel de Unamuno,
in a book that is a single passionate outcry, called "the
tragic sense of life"—*el sentimiento trágico de la vida.*

Unamuno refused to resign himself to death as the end
of individual life. He rejected the consolation of many
religions—spiritual life beyond the grave—and he rejected
the Christian consolation—resurrection of the flesh at the
end of time. He accepted the Christian teachings in the
form of Roman Catholic doctrine because they were bred
into him and because he longed for a faith, but these teachings could not lessen his despair and rebellion. They could
promise and guarantee him another life and the resurrection of his body, but never the continuation of his personality, of his Ego. Neither a spiritual existence nor resur-

rected flesh would be he himself, his living self; nor would
that other world be his world, that in which he was living.
But he wanted, passionately, to remain himself in the flesh
and the world. Anything else would be nothing, or rather
it would be something, but not he. And there was no
remedy. The tragedy of Unamuno was that he had to protest against having to die and yet knew that the annihila-
tion of his personal existence was implacably coming. His
"tragic sense of life" made him equally incapable of
resigning himself to his final death as an individual, and
of deceiving himself so that he could believe in a survival
or resurrection of his individual life.

Nobody can live without shielding his mind from this
searing vision. Unamuno created for himself a double,
indeed a triple, defense. He put his very despair in words
for others, words which carried the imprint of his powerful and unique personality, and which survive. He believed in the continuation through children, through his
own blood. And he held on to the Christian faith, unbeliev-
ing, and believing because he longed to believe. In this
he was like his creation, San Manuel Bueno Martir, the
village priest who could not believe in a life after death
and in a resurrection, but continued to preach the Catholic
faith in an agony of self-negation, so that the others should
go on dreaming and be sheltered from the terrible truth
of death.

Federico García Lorca could not cling to the solution
of procreation, not even for the others. He felt the fearful
greed for survival in the possessive love of mothers for
their children and his mind discovered the inherent frustration: he wrote *Bodas de Sangre* and *Yerma*, in which
death is triumphant precisely through the code of procreation. And Lorca did not even try to mitigate the fear and

terror of individual death by the consolation of religion.
In him the spiritual intimacy with death bred an utter
clarity of vision—"the ice to his song," said Machado—
which heightened his reaction to the living world but for-
bade him to blind himself to the finality of individual
death. His whole work shows that this was his problem:
to live while facing death, and to survive by becoming part
of the surviving world.

Now, the death obsession has been transformed to religious mysticism in so many Spaniards that this mysticism,
in its turn, has influenced the death obsession of other
Spaniards. Loneliness, the "solitude" of the mystics, was
not bearable unless it opened the vista of a new life of the
soul; death, whose existence could never be ignored, had
to be turned into a friend who would open the gate to a
true life; terror and fear of death were converted into a
frenzied contemplation of death and even a longing for
death, to remove its sting. *Me muero porque no muero*—
"I die because I die not"—was the cry of St. Theresa of
Avila. Many have taken this road to escape from their
haunting dread, and the Spanish Church knows only too
well why it keeps the idea and vision of physical death
with its degrading putrefaction so horribly alive in the
minds of its disciples.

But Lorca, with the upbringing, the background, and
the indelible stamp of the Spanish Catholic, has never in
his work shown any trace of having a Catholic, a Christian
faith in resurrection and a life beyond death. His God was
in every created thing, "that center in living flesh, living
cloud, living sea, of Love freed from Time," as he expressed it once in his lecture on the *duende*. Christ was to
him—in the "Ode to the Most Holy Eucharist"—the incarnation of the suffering of creation, the holiness of small,

humble things, and the love which is shelter and order.
But no doctrine, no religious tradition guided his struggle
with the problem of human existence. He fought his death
in life, face to face, without help. And, to quote Unamuno,
le ganó con la verdad de la muerte a la razón de la vida—
"he was gained by the truth of death for the cause of life."

Lorca's struggle against the pattern of life and death
must have begun early, perhaps in his first years when a
grave illness held him paralyzed and released him only
to set him apart from the other children. He seems to have
been lively and playful, but his vitality took the course
of making him enact little plays and conduct religious
services. In the country where he then lived, through his
beloved old nurse or other servants, he may have conceived
the vision of death as the "blanket on the floor" and the oil
lamp at motionless feet. It is possible to imagine that in
his first four years of life, when he could not walk like
the others, a dread of existence permeated his mind; and
that later his reaction was to project himself into an
imagined existence, in motion, worth being lived, and into
an imagined death, worth being died: a heightened life and
a dramatic death. The young boy may have found that he
could make his life more complete and that he could at-
tract or sway others by showing them what they saw so
dimly and he saw so clearly.

I have a feeling that Lorca's constant, ardent interest
in the stage, his great work for *La Barraca,* and also his
puckish texts for marionette plays and Punch-and-Judy
shows, his delight in reciting his own poetry, and his re-
luctance to publish any of his work, may all have something to do with his anxiety to keep alive by making himself come alive to others and by playing with life.

✦

There was only one period in Lorca's life when death, his intimate personal enemy, took on a collective shape in his eyes. Shortly after the stupendous success of his *Romancero Gitano* in Spain, he fled from his private life and, I imagine, from the independent, impersonal life his creation had assumed, leaving him shorn and bereaved of his private public. Lorca went to New York. He did not know English and he did not learn it. The "mechanized jungle" scared him and threatened his poise, even while it thrilled and fascinated him. Life as he understood it, in his own very sheltered existence and in the individual struggle of his Andalusians, was not possible there. He could hardly feel the emotions of the individuals he met, but he felt all the stronger the impact of the multitudes, their cheap joys, their sweat, their greed, their suffering, and their aching emptiness. He smelled corruption and death, the Apocalypse. And Lorca shaped these sensations to a series of poems called *El poeta en Nueva York*, "The Poet in New York," written in 1929-30 and published years after his death.

The work marks a crucial point in Lorca's artistic and intellectual development. To understand it, it is necessary to gauge the depth of the shock he suffered in New York.

There he was, an intensely Spanish Spaniard, oversensitized to the emotions of his own people, but so far untouched by forms of living outside his ken. His people had never been molded by modern industrialism; neither the want nor the caste bondage which weighed upon Spain for centuries had destroyed the individual rhythm of life. Lorca himself, fighting against inexorable individual death in all its shapes, had converted the world of the Andalusian gypsies—*gente con el corazón en la cabeza*, "people with

their hearts in their heads"—into a symbol of quick, innocent life. The visionary world of his poems and plays was
linked to the real, personal life of Spaniards by definite
images and emotions; it was linked to Lorca's own Andalusian soil.

In 1929 this poet from Granada—the landscape of his
mind alive with the silvery green of olive fields, the bright-
ness of whitewashed little houses, with the sound of water
in secret gardens, with the slow movements of sun-drunk
laborers and the proud, unhurried swagger of his gypsies
—finds himself in a street canyon of New York, on a
volcanic floor of asphalt. He had lived in a big city, in
Madrid; yet Madrid is part of the Spanish landscape;
peasants come to market on their small donkeys, the
crooked alleys of the slums belong to the same world as
the village squares; and there is always the profile of the
Sierra under a luminous sky. But in New York the poet
sees only a hustling crowd of people running some-
where—where?—to the shrill sound of klaxons and en-
gine wheels.

He watches the dawn in New York. There is nothing in
it of what he had seen in his country when the first morning lights glittered on roof tiles and windowpanes:

[37]   On the roofs trembled
            little lanterns of tinfoil,
            a thousand glass tambourines
            stabbed through the dawn.

            . . . .

            A long wind left
            in the mouth a rare taste
            of gall, of mint and sweet basil.

In New York he only feels what the dawn is not, and his angry frustration makes the images of his poem abstract and negative:

[38]   Dawn comes and there is no one to receive it in his
            mouth,
        for here is no tomorrow, no possible hope.
        Sometimes minted monies, in furious swarms,
        sting and devour abandoned children.

        The first who come out understand in their bones
        that there will be no paradise, no love unsheathed.
        They know that they go to the mire of rules and
            numbers,
        to games without art, to sweat without fruit.

        The light is entombed in chains and in noises,
        the shameless challenge of a science without roots.
        In the suburbs are people who unslept stagger
        like men just escaped from a bloody shipwreck.

Tortured by the black sorrow of loneliness, he comes back from a walk in the city. But there is nobody of his kind with whom he can share his despair, nobody like "Soledad Montoya" of the "clean and ever lonely sorrow." He only feels that he is one of many living things destroyed by a senseless, vacuous sky; his poetry is immobilized by the shock and can only register broken pieces of reality and broken pieces of images: he is "murdered by the sky" together with the "child of the white egg face" and the "butterfly choked in the inkpot."

Lorca seeks shelter in his childhood and recalls what he then had seen and what he had not seen, as if this would help him to map out the hostile new world:

[39] Those eyes of mine in nineteen hundred and ten
      did not see the dead being buried,
      nor the feast of ashes of someone weeping at dawn,
      nor the heart that trembled, trapped in a hole like
      a sea horse.

The things his boyish eyes had taken in were clearly outlined and concrete, they all had their life, defined by the senses:

      . . . an incomprehensible moon lighting up in the
      corners
      pieces of dried lemon and the hard black of bottles.

      Those eyes of mine on the neck of a filly,
      on the pierced bosom of sleeping Saint Rosa,
      on the roofs of love, with their moons and cool hands,
      on a garden where cats were eating the frogs.

There were palpable objects even in "the place where the dream stumbles over its reality." But in the New York which his eyes of 1929 see he finds only an all-devouring vacuum. Even human beings have no living flesh under their clothes:

      Ask me nothing, I have seen that the things
      seeking their course meet with their void.
      The pain of hollowness is in the unpeopled air
      and in my eyes beings without nudity under their
      clothes!

This sets the keynote to the poems of the whole New York cycle. In a wilderness of cruelly realistic, or bizarre, or enigmatically personal similes, symbols, and images, the poet is seeking "his gaiety and his self" and searching

for other creatures not hollowed out by that mechanized
world which he calls a Senegal with machinery. He takes
refuge with children and tries to recapture with them his
"lost voice." He grapples with fear and loneliness in
poems which map out the "landscape" in a surrealist form
otherwise strange to his lyric. The titles and subtitles are
characteristic: "Landscape of the Mass which Vomits—
Nightfall on Coney Island." "Landscape of the Mass which
Urinates—Nocturne of Battery Square." "City without
Sleep—Nocturne of Brooklyn Bridge."

For a time he can only express in feverish lines his feeling of destruction, of having his vitality and creative
strength drained away from him: "The look that was mine,
but is no longer mine" . . . "I, an armless poet, lost in
the multitude that vomits" . . . or:

[40] I want to cry because I want to,
    as the children cry on the last bench at school,
    because I am neither poet, nor man, nor leaf,
    nothing but a wounded pulse that sounds things from
      beyond.

In the face of the slaughterhouse, symbol of inhuman
mechanized brutality, he rebels and converts his loneliness into an impulse toward another humanity:

[41] Better to weep while the knife is sharpened,
    better to murder dogs in a feverish chase,
    than to bear in the early morning
    the interminable milk trains,
    the interminable blood trains
    and the trains full of roses, manacled
    by manufacturers of perfume.

    . . . .

Every day they kill in New York
four million ducks,
five million pigs,
two thousand pigeons for the pleasure of the mori-
    bund.
. . . .

What shall I do? Arrange the landscapes?
Arrange the loves which then become photos,
which then become chunks of wood and gushes of
    blood?
No, no: I denounce,
I denounce the conspiracy
Of those deserted offices
which transmit no agony. . . .

Then comes the time when Lorca discovers the Negro
of Harlem and believes he has found a static being in a
dynamic world, with a mind still steeped in African dreams,
in his heart a red violence more human than the precision
of timetable, mechanical device, and mass slaughter for
food supplies. Lorca never knew the Negroes of Harlem
as individuals, with countless precise mental associations
such as he was able to give to his stylized gypsies. Nor did
he know their community, with its bitter racial and social
problems. The Negro in his "Ode to the King of Harlem"
is a gigantic symbol of hatred and revolt against the false,
deadening civilization of the city, not a hotel porter in a
garish uniform, with a practical life and a mind full of
personal experiences and dreams. But at the same time
Lorca saw him, saw the Negroes of New York, with the
eyes of a Spanish child. In his infantile dream world the
Negroes were splendid glistening bodies with the movement of panthers, strong enough to send the skyscrapers

crashing. Spanish children of our generation had still seen
Negroes walking in the streets of Madrid or Seville where
they had come in the retinue of wealthy planters or of
generals driven out of the West Indies or the Philippines;
mothers or nurses had still told us thrilling, gruesome
stories of Negro riots, conjuring up pictures of tropical
green and smoking ruins bespattered with blood. These
images, old and new, infantile and intellectual, build up
the vision of the "King of Harlem":

[42] With a spoon
     he scooped out the eyes of the crocodiles
     and spanked the monkeys' bottoms.
     With a spoon.
     . . . .

     Oh, Harlem! Oh, Harlem! Oh, Harlem!
     There is no agony like your oppressed redness,
     like your blood shuddering within your dark eclipse,
     like your garnet violence deaf-and-dumb in the
          shadows,
     like your great King captive in a janitor's suit.
     . . . .
     Negroes, Negroes, Negroes, Negroes.

     The blood has no door in your stretched night.
     There is no blush. The frenzied blood under the skins
     lives on the thorn of the dagger. . . .
     . . . .
     It is the blood that comes, will come over roofs and
          terraces,
     to burn the chlorophyll of the fair women,
     to groan at the foot of beds, before sleepless basins,

and to shatter in an aurora of tobacco and vile yellow.
. . . .
Negroes, Negroes, Negroes, Negroes.

No snake, no goat, no mule ever blanched in death.
The woodcutter does not know when the clamorous
trees which he fells expire.
Wait under the shadow of your overawed King
until hemlock, thistles, and nettles crowd the rear-
    most terraces.
Then, negroes, then, then . . .

For this is his recurring vision: the great rising of all
wild, untamable, suffering, and living things, of plants,
insects, beasts, and unmechanized men, and their storming
of the citadel of money:

[43] And the cobras will hiss in the top stories,
      and the stinging nettles will shake terraces and court-
          yards,
      and the Stock Exchange will be a pyramid of moss,
      and the creepers will come after the rifles,
      and soon, very soon, very soon,
      ah, Wall Street!

But men will claim their right to a human life in peace,
dignity, and tenderness. For the first time Lorca breaks
out in social accusations. In his "Cry toward Rome—from
the Tower of the Chrysler Building" he calls to humiliated
humanity. Love has disappeared from this world, lip-
religion has become sacrilegious. Therefore the humble
people who are still innocent, even if they are caught in
the prison of their daily servitude, must cry out:

[44] . . . the negroes who empty the spittoons,
    the young men trembling under the pale terror of
      the directors,
    the women drowned in mineral oil,
    the multitude of the hammer, the violin or the
      cloud
    . . . .
    must shout with so bold a voice
    that the cities tremble like little girls
    and the prisons of oil and music burst open,
    because we want our daily bread.

Why was it that Lorca saw nothing in the great city beyond baseness and destruction, so that he needed dream visions of conquering jungle plants, avenging Negroes and shouting multitudes to free himself from the tyrannical power of the "deserted offices"?

One of the causes seems to me so simple as to be almost ridiculous: he had to defend his Spanishness in an alien world of which he distrusted sight, sound, and smell. Lorca, like so many others, refused to make himself part of a world other than his own, and thus the new world surrounding him had to be hostile and deadly.

But there was also the deeper reason of his constant personal fight for life. He who defended himself by heightening, not by blurring his sensitiveness, and by transmitting his own vision to others, was suddenly thrown back on his weakness and loneliness in surroundings where his senses were bewildered and dislocated, his vision no longer clear. He had fled from Spain because his work threatened to swallow his personality. Now, in his voluntary exile, despite its fascination and the friendliness which met him and to which he responded eagerly, he saw himself as a shapeless particle in a shapeless mass, his weapons as inadequate as Don Quixote's lance would be in a battle of tanks. He tried to "arrange his landscape"; he had to acknowledge the mass suffering and mass ugliness which he had not recognized on the lesser plane of Spanish society. The shield which had protected him against the impact of social problems splintered. He could no longer give the shape of gypsy lore and Spanish tradition to death and violence. And while his mind was in turmoil he found no clear form, only words, outcries, glimpses of visions, with his old images submerged in the torrent. Hence the rejection of "New York." Hence the surrealist poetry, half intellectual game, half portrait of his inner chaos.

In the end, Lorca went from New York to Cuba as though in flight. The songs of the Negroes there were akin to Moorish songs and to the *flamenco* of Andalusia. R. M. Nadal recalls that Lorca used to say of his arrival in Havana: "I felt as if I had landed in Cadiz." Only then did he regain his poise and see his unrooting experience in perspective. He found his way back to his Spanish form of phrase and rhythm, deliberately, but without the effortless exuberance which before had cloaked his sadness. Something was permanently changed.

When Lorca was back in Spain he did not return to his poetical gypsy world. This way of visualization and identification was closed. From then onward he wrestled with death on a different level in his art. It is as though the confrontation with mass life and mass death had made him both more personal and more impersonal, and certainly more profoundly sad: his poems became more intimate and introspective, his dramatic work more impersonal and searching. The edge of the "silver sickle" had touched his tragedy. It was then that he wrote *Bodas de Sangre, Yerma,* and *Bernarda Alba.*

The shadow deepened when the first upward surge of the new Republic had subsided. Then there was death in the air. Nineteen thirty-four was the year of the rising of the Asturian miners. Lorca may have turned away from the harassing political life, but he could not but feel the currents of violence and desperate hope.

He put his own hopeless, despairing love for life and his hopeless, but by now fearless struggle against the idea of death into the *Lament for Ignacio Sánchez Mejías.* And this poem became the quintessence of the Spanish "tragic sense of life," with roots in the deepest tradition of Spanish poetry.

Ignacio Sánchez Mejías was an Andalusian bullfighter who, after retiring from his profession a wealthy man, returned to the bull ring when he was already mature. He had confidence, rightly, in his experience and courage, though he lacked the perfect physical fitness of youth. But he wanted to escape the gray death "in the blanket" and to conquer death by dying proudly, gallantly. He had been an intimate friend of Lorca's, an unspoiled man of straight and impeccable shape, mentally and physically, and his death hit the poet in his inmost being.

The first part of the *Llanto* expresses nothing but obsession with the fact of the goring and death, *a las cinco de la tarde*—"at five in the afternoon." Like monotonous hammer blows, these words recur after every line:

[45]   At five in the afternoon.
         It was at five sharp in the afternoon.
         A boy brought the white sheet

at five in the afternoon.
A pail of lime, prepared and ready,
at five in the afternoon.
All else was death and only death
at five in the afternoon.

. . . .

When the snowy sweat broke out
at five in the afternoon,
when the bull ring was splashed with iodine
at five in the afternoon,
death hatched her eggs in the wound,
at five in the afternoon,
at five in the afternoon,
at five sharp in the afternoon.

There is a sort of voluptuousness in the insistence on all
the macabre details, on "gangrene approaching," on
"greenish groins," as though the poet wanted to see the
destruction so close that he would lose sight of the dead
friend.

The second part is visionary, laden with symbols taken
from the life of a bullfighter. The poet does not want to see
the blood in the sand. He imagines Ignacio in a dream
world, a dream bull ring, trying to recapture his lost youth
and finding his blood flowing from him—this spilled blood
which the surviving friend does not want to see and cannot
forget.

[46]   I want not to see it!

Tell the moon to come
for I want not to see the blood
of Ignacio on the sand.

I want not to see it!

The moon wide open,
steed of quiet clouds,
and the gray dream bull ring
with willows on the barriers.
I want not to see it!
My remembrance smolders!
Call for the jessamine
with its little whiteness!

I want not to see it!

The cow of the ancient world
passed her sorrowful tongue
over a muzzle of blood
spilled in the sand.
. . . .
I don't want to see it.

Ignacio climbs up the tiers
with his whole death on his shoulders.
He sought for the morning dawn
and there was no morning.
He seeks for his own firm profile
and the dream confuses him.
He sought for his beautiful body
and found his blood flowing.
Don't tell me to see it!
. . . .
His eyes did not close
when he saw the horns looming,

but the terrible mothers
lifted their heads.
And over the cattle ranches
the air filled with secret voices
calling to the bulls of heaven,
herd leaders of pallid mist.

. . . .

Yet now he sleeps without end.
Already the moss and the grasses
open with purposeful fingers
the flower of his skull.
And already his blood comes singing,
singing across marshes and meadows,
sliding off chill, stiff horns,
reeling soulless through the mist,
stumbling over a thousand hooves,
like a long, dark, woeful tongue,
to gather in a pool of agony
by the Guadalquivir of the stars.
Oh white wall of Spain—
Oh black bull of anguish—
Oh Ignacio's strong blood—
Oh nightingale of his veins!
No.
I want not to see it!
There is no chalice that would hold it,
there are no swallows that could drink it,
no rimefrost of light to cool it,
no chant and no torrent of lilies,
no crystal to cover it with silver.
No.
I do not want to see it!!

Federico, the poet, saw his strong friend battling with the laws of life, fighting to find again "his own firm profile," the effortless poise of youth. But the fight went against him, although his life had been courageous, gentle, and limpid, his head "a golden glow of Andalusian Rome," his hands soft on young wheat and dew, his muscles hard when he spurred his horse. There was to be the inescapable ending: the "ordeal by grass," the slow corruption of the flesh which the poet hated to remember, yet could never forget, and which no ritual or religious myth, no chalice, hymn, or symbolic lily wreath could exorcise.

Then the body, still real and "present," is laid out on the marble slab, and the poet wants to make it clear to himself what this means. In the third part of the Lament— *Cuerpo Presente*, "Body Present"—he tries to think out the mystery of death of which he knows no solution:

[47] Now Ignacio the well born lies on the stone.
      Now it is finished. What is it? Look at his face:
      Death has covered it with sulphurous pallor
      and given him the head of a dark minotaur.
      . . . .
      What is it they say? Heavy with stench rests the
         silence.
      We are with a laid-out body that evanesces,
      with a clear shape that had nightingales once,
      and we see it get pitted with bottomless holes.
      . . . .
      I want to see here the men with hard voices,
      those who break horses and harness the rivers,
      the men whose bones resound and who sing
      with mouths full of sun and of flint stone.

Here I want to see them. Before this stone.
Before this body with broken reins.
I want them to show me where the way out
exists for this captain shackled by death.
. . . .
I do not want them to cover his face with a handker-
   chief
that he may become used to the death he carries.
Go, Ignacio. Do not heed the hot bellow.
Sleep, fly, rest. Even the sea dies.

What is it that happens? asks the poet. Nobody can
show the way out, the solution, not even the strongest, the
men whose bodies are imbued with sunlight and whose
teeth are glistening-hard as flint. There is no consolation
for the man who died, undaunted but defeated, and there
is no argument his friend could accept but the one that
this is the tremendous fate of everything alive: even the
sea dies.

There is the echo of very old Spanish poetry and tradition in these verses, but their spirit is different. It is in-
effably sad, because it knows of no mystic salvation. Old
Jorge Manrique also associated death and the sea:

> Our lives are the rivers
> that end in the sea
> which is death. . . .

But to this poet of the fifteenth century the end of individual life was the beginning of another life, and the
common fate of mankind was death and resurrection. To
Lorca the individual end is final. And he forces himself to
face it in all its cruel finality, because with this knowledge

—which excludes any death wish—life must be lived out courageously and gaily.

The last part of the poem—*Alma Ausente*, "Soul Absent"—recognizes the victory of death and at the same time Ignacio's ultimate victory over death through his clear and beautiful life. It lifts up the courage of the living by showing them what they can do: face death, remember the dead, and carry on the chain of life, doomed conquerors.

[48]   Neither the bull nor the fig tree knows you any more,
          nor the horses, nor the ants in your house.
          Neither the child nor the evening knows you any
               more,
          because you have died forever.
          . . . .
          The autumn will come with empty sea shells,
          with misty grapes and serried mountains,
          but no one will want to look into your eyes,
          because you have died forever.

          Because you have died forever,
          like all the dead of the Earth,
          like all the dead who are forgotten
          as in a heap of muted dogs.

          No one knows you any more. No. But I sing you.
          I sing for later times your profile and your grace.
          The noble maturity of your wisdom.
          Your longing for Death and the taste of Her mouth,
          the sadness that lay in your valient gaiety. . . .

This *apetencia de muerte*, the "longing for death," is something different from the mental attitude called "death

wish," because in the sense of Lorca's verse it means the
meeting with death as an act of conscious assertion of life.
But it is a heavy burden, and it contains the dangerous
contradiction, the dualism, of Spanish spiritual values.

Cyril Connolly touched on this problem in *Enemies of
Promise,* written in 1938:

> The Spanish poet Lorca was shot because he
> fell into the power of an element which detested
> spiritual reality. Yet Lorca fell into that power
> because he lived in Granada. Had he lived in
> Barcelona or Madrid he would be alive today
> like Sender or Alberti. But he lived in reaction-
> ary Granada, a city of the past, of gipsies and
> bullfighters and priests, and he made his best
> poems about bullfighters and gipsies. That ele-
> ment in him which sought the past, which drew
> him to the mediaevalism of Andalusia, contained
> the seed of his own death, placing him, who was
> no friend to priests or feudal chiefs, in a city
> where the past one day came to life, and was
> deadly.

Not two years after the death of the bullfighter Sánchez
Mejías the sadness in Federico's own "valiant gaiety" was
fulfilled. Whether those who murdered him were Civil
Guards or Falangists or simple gunmen of fascism, they
were fitting representatives of the deadening element
against which Lorca had always fought, even in himself
and even when he felt it part of himself. We know no detail of his assassination, except that it happened in the
early hours of morning. But how could his lifelong fight
against death have ended otherwise than in his dying without fear?

✦

After all this it must be obvious that Lorca's death-defying poetry has a particular effect on his Spanish readers, an effect produced not by the words but by the associations they carry. Those words speak of the sadness and terror of death. But since all Spaniards, more or less clearly but always consciously, possess their own philosophy of death, Lorca's courage in facing the issue without any softening veil provokes a clarifying reaction in their minds: it spurs them to dominate death, to be greater than death itself. It tells them that, with or without a future life, with or without a Supreme Judge, with or without the physical horrors of death, it is possible for a man to die so that he kills his own death. And thus Lorca tells them that they must live a clean and upright life, not cringing before death, yet not forgetting the unforgettable.

THE POET AND HIS ART

The artist is exceptional in that he is an absolute creator: a creator first of new concepts, then of new forms to express them, and finally, through both original concept and form, creator of new esthetic sensations in the minds of others. Thus the artist becomes a phenomenon—or a miracle—through his work.

We all, including the artist, want to discover the secret which worked the miracle of art that moves us, as though possession of this secret would turn the critic into a creative artist, the reader into a potential artist, and as though the artist himself would then get rid of the ache of creating and of the nagging fear of failure.

Lorca, an exceptional and original artist, has not escaped the general rule. His work has been examined and taken to pieces by critics and readers; a considerable number of volumes attempting to define the secret of his art have been published. Lorca, too, has tried to explain himself, perhaps from an urge to overcome the helpless feeling that his art at its greatest was something outside himself, outside his conscious effort.

Federico García Lorca has often been called an "unconscious" poet and a great improviser, because he was so clearly not a cerebral writer and because the poems he seemed to improvise as he recited them had an immense freshness and charm. Neither of the two labels fits. Before the inspired vision became final poetic form and art, he brought his whole culture, craftsmanship, and intellectual integrity to the work, knowing that they could either extinguish or nurse the initial spark, although they could neither replace nor provide the divine fire.

In the foregoing pages I have tried to describe the great quarry from which Lorca took his raw material. Now I want to show how he himself understood his processing, the transformation of the material into limited, proportioned forms, how his ideas became flesh in his poems, and how he attempted to express the mystery of art to others and to himself.

In 1927, when Spain commemorated the three-hundredth anniversary of the death of Luis de Góngora, the greatest Spanish Baroque poet and the one who rouses most controversy, Federico García Lorca gave the memorial address at Granada. It became a profession of faith. Defining Góngora's artistry and the process by which he created his metaphors, Lorca explained the principles of poetic creation as he understood them at the time; identifying himself with the other Andalusian poet whom professors of literature conventionally praised for his easy "popular" verse and condemned for his obscure "cultured" poetry, he expressed his own artistic problems.

In this lecture he showed his belief in relentless intellectual work to give an inspired image its valid form. The poet, he said, has to "chase" the poem he conceives through the maze of his imagination; he must not fall for artifice or for false metaphors or for facile solutions; he must— like Góngora—organize the landscape of his poem by analyzing its components. It is not enough to capture an inspiration:

> The great French poet Paul Valéry says that the state of inspiration is not that in which to write a poem. As I believe in the inspiration God sends, I believe that Valéry is on the right track. The state of inspiration is one of withdrawal, not of creative dynamism. The vision of a concept must be left to settle so as to clarify. I believe that no great writer works in a state of fever. . . . One returns from inspiration as though from a foreign country, and the poem is the description of the journey in that country. Inspiration supplies the image but not its clothing. And to clothe it, it is necessary to observe the quality and sound of each word, calmly and without any dangerous exaltation.

How to become "absolute master of one's reality" like Góngora? The poet has to limit himself. He has to "examine his conscience and study the mechanism of his creation with all his critical capacity." A year before the lecture on Góngora he had written in his "Ode to Salvador Dali": "A desire for limit and form invades us." In his intellectual crisis he defined the limits he set himself and explained the essence of his—though not of Góngora's—imagery:

> A poet must be a Professor of the five bodily senses. Of the five senses, in the following order: sight, touch, hearing, smell, and taste. To command the most perfect images, he must open doors of communication between all of the

senses. . . . The metaphor is always ruled by
vision, though at times by a sublimated vision;
it is the vision, too, which limits a metaphor and
gives it reality. It does not permit a shadow to
blur the outlines of an image it has seen clearly
drawn. . . . All images are born in the visual
field. The metaphor links two antagonistic worlds
through an equestrian leap of imagination.

This, then, was Lorca's conception of imaginative poetry:
however bold a metaphor or the images which went into
its making, it had to have a kernel of sensual experience,
of realistic observation. He obeyed his own rule most
faithfully. Or perhaps the opposite is true: he came to
formulate this rule intellectually because his creative
mechanism was of this particular nature.

Equally, it was an echo of Lorca's way of "chasing
images" when he observed of Góngora:

He combines astronomic sensations with the
tiny details of the infinitely small. . . . So an
apple and an ocean are the same to him, for he
knows that the apple is as infinite as the sea,
each within its world. The life of an apple from
the time when it is a delicate flower to the moment when, golden-russet, it drops from the tree
into the grass is as mysterious and as great as
the perpetual rhythm of the tides. And a poet
must know this. . . . Góngora treats all his
matters with the same measure and analyzes
fruit or objects as he handles, with cyclopean
strength, seas and continents. Even more: he de-
lights more fervently in the small things.

Lorca did not "handle" mythological islands and seas like Góngora, who brought into his poetic landscape the whole Olympus and the exciting geography of his age, when America was a "new-found land." But the Baroque poet from Cordova and the modern poet from Granada shared the Andalusian love for gemlike, limited beauty— the beauty of a small animal like a bee or a frog, and the beauty of a fruit, a branch, a flower—which is as much part of the Hispano-Moorish heritage as the love for fountains, streams, and pools set among the trees of a walled garden.

In a prose piece entitled "Granada, Paradise Closed to Many," Lorca gave a psychological explanation for the love of the diminute and the use of the colloquial diminutive which in his opinion characterizes the speech of Granada to an even greater extent than that of the rest of Andalusia:

> The only mission of the diminutive is to limit and compress things and ideas with a great perspective, to bring them into our room, within our grasp. The diminutive limits time, space, the sea, the moon, the distances, and even that marvel—action. We do not want the world to be so very great, nor the sea so very deep. There is a need to confine, to domesticate the immeasurable terms.

His own verse confirmed that there was a spiritual need behind his urge to express the ineffable in limited pictures. So the "Ode to the Most Holy Eucharist," one of the most abstract of his poems, published in 1928:

[49] You were alive, my God in the monstrance,
     pierced with needles of light by your Father,
     palpitating like the poor heart of a frog
     which the doctors put in a glass jar.
    . . . .
     It is thus I want to have you, God on show,
     little flour wafer for the newborn child. . . .

Lorca's poetic reality, with its emotional roots and its sustained double vision of the tangible and the symbolic world, was fundamentally different from Góngora's. Precisely for this reason he was able to use the example of Góngora for a clarification of his own intellectual process, at a time when he went through a crisis and reached out for new forms of expression. Other poets of his generation learned from Góngora's technique to the point that the influence of his style sapped their originality and became a recipe, together with the theories of French "pure" poetry; Lorca learned about himself from Góngora. The Spanish-American poet Pablo Neruda once wrote:

> Among the brilliant generation of poets such as Alberti, Aleixandre, Altolaguirre, Cernuda, etc., he [Lorca] was perhaps the only one on whom the shade of Góngora did not have that icy hold which aesthetically paralyzed the great young poetry of Spain in 1927.

Certainly the analytical process behind Góngora's work was alien to Lorca, stimulating though it was for him. All through his lecture he went to the core of his own poetic ideas and on the way recognized most sharply those ele-

ments in Góngora which corresponded to a problem or a
need he himself felt.

It was his own problem that he stated when he tried to
explain why Góngora had abandoned his successful popular style and turned to new, ornate, deliberately unreal
forms:

> What reason may Góngora have had for
> launching his lyrical revolution? Reasons? . . .
> They have to be found not in history, but in his
> soul. . . . The need for a new kind of beauty,
> and the boredom which the poetical production
> of his time caused him, developed in him an
> acute, nearly unbearable critical sensitiveness.
> He began almost to hate poetry. . . . He was
> no longer able to create poems smacking of the
> old Castilian style. . . . All the dust of Castile
> weighed on his soul and on the folds of his seer's
> mantle. . . . Tired of Castile and of "local
> color" . . .

Lorca's *Romancero Gitano* had not yet been published,
though some of its ballads were already famous. He re-
belled against the fate which threatened him, that of being
tied to an "old Andalusian style" and classified as a poet
of "local color." He had used his dream-gypsies as an
objectivized link between the concrete world his senses
grasped and the visionary world of his mind that he expressed in symbols. Now he wanted to widen his range,
to sift his images. At the stage before his escape from the
"dust of Castile" to the challenging new world of New
York, an objective, theoretical survey of his art had become an intimate necessity for him.

But even while he experimented with abstract lyrics and
surrealist drama, and while he accepted an intellectual

approach to art in his desire for clarification, limitation, and selection, he never denied the mainspring of his imagery: the reality of his senses and feelings which he shared with his people. In the same lecture where he stressed that "of course" Góngora did not create his images directly from nature, but transformed them in the "darkroom of his mind," Lorca explained the close link between observed nature, popular similes, and poetic image in his own mind:

> A poetical image is always a transference of meaning. Any language consists of images, and that of our people has an immense wealth of them. . . . To call one confection "Heaven's Bacon" and another "Nun's Sigh" is to create two delightful and yet acute images; the same is true of the expression "half-orange," for a cupola, and so forth. In Andalusia popular imagery reaches astounding depths of penetration and sensitiveness, it achieves transmutations much like Góngora's. Thus they call a deep watercourse that flows slowly through the fields "an ox of water," to indicate its volume and mighty harnessed strength. And I have heard a farmer from Granada say: "The rushes love to grow on the tongue of the river." These are two images created by the people closely corresponding to Góngora's style.

Even the samples from Andalusian folklore here quoted belong not to Góngora's poetry, where flashes of sensual imagery were but the counterfoil of the erudite, recondite metaphor he cultivated, but to Lorca's work.

The following lines occur in the "Ballad of the Summoned Gypsy Amargo":

[50]   The dense water oxen
         rush at the boys
         who bathe in the moons
         of their wavy horns.
         . . . .
         It will happen at night, in the dark,
         in the magnetized mountains,
         where the water oxen drink
         the rushes, dreaming.

Lorca must have fallen in love with these two popular images, that of the slow, strong water oxen, and that of the rushes being fond of the licking tongue of the rivers (the "oxen"), because he was not content with having transformed them into poetry, but had to define them in intellectual terms afterward. He had seen the running water and the rushes through his own eyes and through the eyes of his people; he had made the image his own; and then he "threw doors of communication" wide open. In his poem the water oxen live their life, parallel to the life of the water, yet on another plane: they strike at the bathing boys with their horns—rippling waves which a silvery light turns into shining moon sickles—and in the quiet darkness of the night they are dreamily lapping at the rushes with their tongues.

Here Lorca had fulfilled the esthetic demand which he developed at a later stage, when he discussed the mechanism of Góngora's art: born in the visual field, limited and clearly confined by the underlying observation of reality, his metaphors link the antagonistic worlds of "animate" and "inanimate" life and create a new, haunting reality.

✦

In some of Lorca's poems the image is so condensed,
the visual impression on which it draws so strictly limited
to Spanish life, that it sounds fantastic or surrealist in
translation, though it is a severely constructed, lucid symbol of a common experience. An example of this is a verse
from the "*Casida* of the Clear Death" which I have already
quoted:

[*see* 27]
> There is no one who in giving a kiss
> does not feel the smile of the faceless people,
> no one who, touching a newborn child,
> can forget the motionless horse skulls.

The meaning of the verse is obvious enough: the implacable nearness of death felt at the touch of beloved living flesh. The grin of the jaws of a death-head—the "smile
of the faceless people"—is one of the oldest symbols for
the vanity of life; spiritual exercises as universal as the
Catholic Church make the mental association between
warm, kissed lips and the hidden skull underneath almost
inescapable. The obsession with death ("There is *no one*
who . . . does not feel . . . *no one* who . . . can forget . . .") is Lorca's personal expression of the familiar-
ity with death bred into Spaniards. But what about the
"motionless horse skulls"? Are they the skulls in one of
Salvador Dali's landscapes? A purely private symbol?
A frightening nightmare?

Many Spaniards will recognize the concrete vision behind this condensed image, for it is part and parcel of
their lives. Two or three miles from countless villages in
the Castilian and above all the Andalusian plains there is

a ravine in which the bleached skulls of horses, mules, and donkeys are piling up. It is a mass grave of domestic animals, visited by carrion birds. The people of those villages, and others like myself who happened to stay there with relatives, pass through various stages of an almost philosophical relationship with those graveyards. As small children they live in terror of the skulls; as growing boys they try to get rid of their childish fear by playing pranks with the bones; as men they may throw into the pit the body of a horse of whom they were fond, and mumble the traditional formula: "And so we all end!" To anyone who has the picture of such a ravine at the back of his memory Lorca's dark phrase of the "motionless horse skulls" will be translucent. It will move him with the submerged power of an old, shared emotion and open his mind to the mood and thought of the poem.

One of the most famous ballads of the *Romancero Gitano*, the *Romance Sonámbulo*, recited to the point of becoming hackneyed by Spaniards who intoxicate themselves with its words, opens with four lines whose sound is music, while the meaning is elusive. Hearers or readers are prone to take those lines as a mere sound painting of the "somnambulant" mood. In this case it is important to see the original text together with a word-by-word translation. Here are both:

> *Verde que te quiero verde.*
> *Verde viento. Verdes ramas.*
> *El barco sobre la mar*
> *y el caballo en la montaña.*

> Green, I want you green.
> Green wind. Green boughs.

The ship on the sea
and the horse in the mountains.

The music of the Spanish verse turns on the sound of
the word for green—*verde*—with its two syllables, and on
the change of stress at the end of the third line, through
the only monosyllabic key word. There is nothing of this
particular melody in the English translation. I imagine
however (though I cannot be certain of it in the way an
English writer would be certain of an effect) that something of the mystery and simplicity of the original comes
through the familiar English words: green—wind—boughs
—ship—sea—horse—mountains. They could not be simpler, those words, either in Spanish or English. Yet behind their puzzling bareness lies a complex, definite picture condensing the emotions which carry the action of the
ballad.

This is the action: The gypsy girl who lives in the hot
yellow plain, in her father's house with its flat roof and
its cistern pool, is in love with a smuggler whose trade
sends him on horseback over the hills to the sea where at
night the ship with contraband comes to the shore. On his
return he has to elude the customs officers and the Civil
Guard who shoot on sight. She has been waiting for him
in vain during many nights, leaning over the rail of the
roof-terrace and staring at the hills, into the moon, into
the green weeds of the cistern below, which throws a faint
greenish glow back onto her face. Her longing for her
lover grows into an obsession embracing everything that
stands for him: the sea, the green hills, the moist wind
from sea and hills, the richness, gentleness, and fulfillment
of a lush green world where there is no thirst and frustra-

tion. In the end, when her whole being is entranced in that longed-for green world, while in her concrete, real world

[51]   under the gypsy moon
the things are looking at her
and she cannot look at them,

she throws herself into the cistern pool, a sleepwalker following the green glow. Her lover, mortally wounded by his pursuers, drags himself to her house, there to die "decently in a bed." He is too late. She is dead. The Civil Guard knock at the door.

The melodramatic part of the action, the story of the wounded smuggler—theme of innumerable folk songs in all languages—is told through a dialogue between the two gypsies, the smuggler himself and the girl's father. It uses the dramatic similes and flowered idioms of Andalusian folk tradition in a poetically heightened form. Thus the father speaks of the wound in the lover's breast and tries to tell him of the suicide of his daughter:

[51 cont.]
Three hundred dark roses
spread over your white shirt.
Your blood smells and oozes
around your sash.
But I am no more my self
and my house is no more my house. . . .

Here the poetry is rooted in folk legend, the images are popular images. But intertwined with and superimposed on this part of the action runs the "somnambulant" story, the inner action condensed in the first four lines, with their

And the mountain, furtive
is bristling its acrid
cactus

"green" dream words and with the flashlike picture of
movement and freedom: ship on the sea, horse in the mountains. The dream tension is carried on in the vision of the
landscape:

[51 cont.]

> Green, I want you green.
> Big rimefrost stars
> come with the shadow fish
> that opens the path of dawn.
> The fig tree rubs its belly
> with the rasp of its branches
> and the mountain, a thieving cat,
> bristles its angry spikes.

*Great stars of frost
come with the
fish
of
shadow
that opens
the
road
of
dawn*

It is a perfect evocation of the hour before dawn. The
low stars which begin to grow and glitter frostily, the misty
shadow floating in the east, the sudden chill wind which
rustles the trees, the black, crouching outline of the hills
where the spiky agave plants are suddenly visible against
a paling sky, are each given identity and life in pictures
as sensually direct as if a child had invented them in one
of its monologues. The gypsies of the Andalusian plain
might use every one of these images in their vivid tales.
But the poem has woven them into a pattern which opens
those "doors of communication" between the senses and
sustains the double reality, that of the real world and that
of the dream world which is not less real. And it is the
imagined reality which tells the inner story, the story of
longing for a green world, that never ends, not even when
the gypsy girl floats on the green surface of the pool, in
the last cold glint of the moon, and the brutality of the
outer world knocks at the gate:

*The fig tree is
chafing its wind
with the sandpaper of its
branches*

[51 cont.]

An icicle of moonlight
supports her on the water.

The night grew intimate
like a little square.
Drunken Civil Guards
were beating on the door.
Green, I want you green.
Green wind. Green boughs.
The ship on the sea.
And the horse in the mountains.

Is it possible to explain rationally the power which turns a chain of simple, well-worn words into magic? All that can be done is to discover some of the roots of the poet's creation, to single out some of the chords it strikes, to give a glimpse of the world it reveals to those who shared the reality it transforms. And this is not enough.

The poet Rafael Alberti, speaking of the first time he had heard Federico García Lorca recite his "Somnambulant Ballad," has said: "His 'green wind' touched us all, leaving its echo in our ears."

This sentence says more than a dozen definitions. In the end, the work of art is not summed up by the artist's mastery of his matter, the perfection of its shape, the associations it rouses, and the pleasure it confers. Beyond the achievements of craftsmanship, often without such achievements, there is the living breath of the work of art, the spirit which touches and shakes us.

As an intelligent, conscious craftsman Lorca could explain the mechanism of images, poetic transformation, and evasion, the rules to be learned from traditional and modern sources. He could insist on the value of experiments with every imaginable form from surrealist drama to marionette plays in eighteenth-century style, from Arabic *casidas* and *ghaseels* to the exacting architecture of sonnets, with the simple or erudite, long or short words each stress and shift demands in the right place. It would be possible, and interesting, to study Lorca's vocabulary and the origin of symbols and sound groups he used again and again: his green wind, meadow, moon, river, and sea; anemone, dahlia, oleander, jessamine, and bitter root; frogs, bulls, and ants; the intrusion of metal, of nickel, silver, or knife, into his dream landscapes. It would be fairly easy in his case to define literary influences, because they were soon absorbed and transformed, and less important than in most other writers of his time and country. Some of all this has been done, much more will no doubt be done.

And yet, when it comes to the essence of art, analysis falls short. Leonardo da Vinci's scientific rules of proportion do not "explain" the smile of his Mona Lisa. There remains Lorca's own way, the metaphor and allegory in which he invoked the elusive spirit without violating it.

In Lorca's lecture on the *duende* in 1930, to which I have referred several times, he was concerned with the spirit of art, not with its method as in the lecture on Góngora. Since then he had passed through his mental crisis and saw the intellectual part of an artist's work in proportion to the whole. "The artist," he now said, "climbs every new stair in the tower of his perfection by paying for it in his struggle with the daemon [the *duende*], not with an angel as has been said, nor with the muse."

The "angel" is in his interpretation a grace from above

which guides and endows, prohibits, prevents and warns, so that the artist achieves his work effortlessly. The "muse" dictates or at least whispers into the poet's ear, it wakes his intellect. But "the intellect is often the enemy of poetry, because it imitates too much, because it sets him on a sharp-edged throne and makes him forget that suddenly the ants may devour him." The poet who follows a purely intellectual inspiration with its tempting vistas and "false taste of laurels" too easily neglects the darker forces before which mannerisms and fashions are powerless. (Góngora, whose cold strength of artistry Lorca admired and used as a whetstone at an earlier stage, is here quoted as a poet ruled by the "muse.")

Then Lorca sums up his allegory:

> Angel and muse come from without. The angel gives light, the muse gives forms . . . golden bread or folds of the tunic; the poet receives rules in his shrubbery of laurels. Yet the daemon has to be wakened in the ultimate recesses of the blood. It means to reject the angel and kick out the muse. To shed all awe of the fragrance of violets which eighteenth-century poetry exhales, and all awe of the great telescope in whose lenses the muse falls asleep, sick of limits. The true struggle is with the *duende*, the daemon.

Characteristically Lorca took his Spanish term for daemonic inspiration from the Andalusian idiom. While to the rest of Spain the *duende* is nothing but a hobgoblin, to Andalusia it is an obscure power which can speak through every form of human art, including the art of personality. A performer can infuse an insipid piece of hackneyed music with his or her *duende*, and turn it into truth and beauty. A dancer can give stirring power to a ritual gesture. A bullfighter can transform the mathematical rules of space and the feats of masculine courage which belong to the stylized play with death in the bull ring, so that he creates beauty and emotion charged with the knowledge of human limits transgressed. The raucous cries of the Andalusian "Deep Song" come from the depths of the human heart where the anguish of all creation is hidden, and their singers have to forget all technical tricks, they have to make their voices sound like gushes of blood, if they want to release the *duende*. Whenever and wherever a human being, great artist and little performer alike, is possessed of the daemon, the Andalusian people with their unerring feeling for the "dark root of the cry," to repeat Lorca's words, respond to it. Everything else falls flat.

To explain the "daemon" which to him was the spirit of truest art, Lorca used examples from popular life. There was the old gypsy dancer who on hearing a fragment of Bach exclaimed: *"Olé,* that has got *duende!"* There was the Andalusian who said of a nocturne by Falla: "Everything that has black sounds has *duende."* There was the dancing competition in Jerez de la Frontera where an eighty-year-old woman, after a display by beautiful or charming young dancers, won the first prize, doing nothing but lift her arms, fling back her head, and beat the dais with her foot—with the power of a dying *duende.* Then he spoke of artists with great names who at times wrestled with the daemon in them and "kicked aside" their perfect technical skill: Velázquez who escaped from the princely grays of his portraits when the spirit rode him, Goya who dropped his exquisite rose-and-silver tones and scratched horrible pitch-black visions on the walls of his house. Most of the names he quoted are Spanish, for the daemon means awareness of death, and to Lorca's mind Spain more than any other country listens incessantly for the "black sounds."

But every art and country has its own daemon. It happens—it cannot be manufactured—when old forms have been radically transmuted, old rules broken and remade, and the new creation is imbued with the freshness and wonder of another beginning, yet still marked by the struggle with the fear of death.

"The daemon inflicts a wound," said Lorca, "and in the cure of this wound which never closes lies the uncommon, the inventive quality of a man's work. The magic virtue of a poem consists in being always daemon-ridden so that it baptizes with dark water those who look at it. . . . The daemon? Where is the daemon?"

The answer comes back from this man's work:

> Let them seek you on my brow,
> play of moon and of sand.

APPENDIX

SPANISH TEXT OF QUOTATIONS

[1] Fue un tiempo de mentira, de infamia. A España toda,
     la malherida España, de Carnaval vestida
     nos la pusieron, pobre y escuálida y beoda,
     para que no acertara la mano con la herida.

     Fué ayer; éramos casi adolescentes; era
     con tiempo malo, encinta de lúgubres presagios,
     cuando montar quisimos en pelo una quimera,
     mientras la mar dormía ahita de naufragios.

     Dejamos en el puerto la sórdida galera,
     y en una nave de oro nos plugo navegar
     hacia los altos mares, sin aguardar ribera,
     lanzando velas y anclas y gobernalle al mar.

     Ya entonces, por el fondo de nuestro sueño—herencia
     de un siglo que vencido sin gloria se alejaba—
     un alba entrar quería; con nuestra turbulencia
     la luz de las divinas ideas batallaba.

     Mas cada cual el rumbo siguió de su locura;
     agilitó su brazo, acreditó su brio;

dejó como un espejo bruñida su armadura
y dijo: "El hoy es malo, pero el mañana . . . es
mío."

Y es hoy aquel mañana de ayer. . . . Y España
toda,
con sucios oropeles de Carnaval vestida
aun la tenemos: pobre y escuálida y beoda;
mas hoy de un vino malo: la sangre de su herida.

Tú, juventud más joven, si de más alta cumbre
la voluntad te llega, irás a tu aventura
despierta y transparente a la divina lumbre,
como el diamante clara, como el diamante pura.

Una España joven—ANTONIO MACHADO, 1914

[2]   De los cuatro muleros
                                 que van al agua,
                                 el de la mula torda
                                 me roba el alma.

                                 De los cuatro muleros
                                 que van al río,
                                 el de la mula torda
                                 es mi marío.

                                 ¿A qué buscas la lumbre
                                 la calle arriba
                                 si de tu cara sale
                                 la brasa viva?

[3]   Los caballos negros son,
                                 las herraduras son negras.

Sobre las capas relucen
manchas de tinta y de cera.
Tienen, por eso no lloran,
de plomo las calaveras.
Con el alma de charol
vienen por la carretera.
Jorobados y nocturnos,
por donde animan ordenan
silencios de goma obscura
y miedos de fina arena.
Pasan, si quieren pasar,
y ocultan en la cabeza
una vaga astronomía
de pistolas inconcretas.

Romance de la Guardia Civil española

[4]   Cuando llegaba la noche
noche que noche nochera
los gitanos en sus fraguas
forjaban soles y flechas.

. . . .

La Virgen y San José
perdieron sus castañuelas,
y buscan a los gitanos
para ver si las encuentran.
La Virgen viene vestida
con un traje de Alcaldesa,
de papel de chocolate
con los collares de almendras.
San José mueve los brazos
bajo una capa de seda.

. . . .

Estandartes y faroles
invaden las azoteas.
Por los espejos sollozan
bailarinas sin caderas.
Agua y sombra, sombra y agua
por Jerez de la Frontera.

¡Oh ciudad de los gitanos!
En las esquinas, banderas.
Apaga tus verdes luces
que viene la benemérita.
. . . .
Avanzan de dos en fondo
a la ciudad de la fiesta.
Un rumor de siemprevivas
invade las cartucheras.
Avanzan de dos en fondo.
Doble nocturno de tela.
El cielo se les antoja
una vitrina de espuelas.

La ciudad, libre de miedo,
multiplicaba sus puertas.
Cuarenta guardias civiles
entran a saco por ellas.
Los relojes se pararon,
y el coñac de las botellas
se disfrazó de noviembre
para no infundir sospechas.
Un vuelo de gritos largos
se levantó en las veletas.
Los sables cortan las brisas
que los cascos atropellan.

Por las calles de penumbra
huyen las gitanas viejas
con los caballos dormidos
y las orzas de moneda.
. . . .
Pero la Guardia Civil
avanza sembrando hogueras,
donde joven y desnuda
la imaginación se quema.
Rosa la de los Camborios
gime sentada en su puerta
con sus dos pechos cortados
puestos en una bandeja.
. . . .
Cuando todos los tejados
eran surcos en la tierra,
el alba meció sus hombros
en largo perfil de piedra.

¡Oh, ciudad de los gitanos!
La Guardia Civil se aleja
por un túnel de silencio
mientras las llamas te cercan.

¡Oh, ciudad de los gitanos!
¿Quién te vió y no te recuerda?
Que te busquen en mi frente.
Juego de luna y arena.
          Romance de la Guardia Civil española

[5]   . . . El Juez, con Guardia Civil,
          por los olivares viene.

Sangre resbalada gime
muda canción de serpiente.

—Señores Guardias Civiles:
aquí pasó lo de siempre.
Han muerto cuatro romanos
y cinco cartagineses.

Reyerta

[6]   La noche se puso íntima
como una pequeña plaza.
Guardias Civiles borrachos
en la puerta golpeaban. . . .

Romance sonámbulo

[7]   Veinticuatro bofetadas,
veinticinco bofetadas;
después, mi madre, a la noche,
me pondrá en papel de plata.

Guardia Civil caminera,
dadme unos sorbitos de agua.
Agua con peces y barcos.
Agua, agua, agua, agua.

¡Ay, mandor de los civiles
que estás arriba en tu sala!
¡No habrá pañuelos de seda
para limpiarme la cara!

Canción del gitano apaleado

[8]   El campo
de olivos

se abre y se cierra
como un abanico.
Sobre el olivar
hay un cielo hundido
y una lluvia obscura
de luceros fríos.
Tiembla junco y penumbra
a la orilla del río.
Se riza el aire gris.
Los olivos
están cargados
de gritos.
Una bandada
de pájaros cautivos,
que mueven sus larguísimas
colas en lo sombrío.

Poema de la Siguiriya gitana—Paisaje

[9] . . . Quiero tener abiertos mis balcones al sol
para que llene el suelo de flores amarillas
y quererte, segura de tu amor, sin que nadie
me aceche . . .
. . . .
Yo bordé la bandera por él. Yo he conspirado
para vivir y amar su pensamiento propio.
Más que a mis propios hijos y a mí misma le quise.
¿Amas la Libertad más que a tu Marianita?
¡Pues yo seré la misma Libertad que tú adoras!
. . . .
Mis hijos llevarán resplandor en el rostro
que no podrán borrar los años ni los aires!
Si delato, por todas las calles de Granada

este nombre sería pronunciado con miedo.

. . . .

Pedro, quiero morir
por lo que tú no mueres,
por el puro ideal que iluminó tus ojos:

. . . .

En mis últimas horas yo quiero engalanarme.
Quiero sentir la dura caricia de mi anillo
y prenderme en el pelo mi mantilla de encaje.
Amas la libertad por encima de todo,
pero yo soy la mísma Libertad. Doy mi sangre,
que es tu sangre y la sangre de todas las criaturas.
¡No se podrá comprar el corazón de nadie!

. . . .

¡Yo soy la libertad porque el amor lo quiso!
¡Pedro! La Libertad, por la cual me dejaste.
¡Yo soy la Libertad herida por los hombres!
Amor, amor, amor y eternas soledades!

. . . .

Hay un miedo que da miedo.
Las calles están desiertas.
Solo el viento viene y va.
Pero la gente se encierra.

. . . .

No habrá nadie en Granada que se asome
cuando usted pase con su comitiva.
Los andaluces hablan, pero luego . . .

Mariana Pineda

[10]   Cuando se abre en la mañana,
              roja como sangre está.
              El rocío no la toca
              porque se teme quemar.

Abierta en el medio día
es dura como el coral.
El sol se asoma a los vidrios
para verla relumbrar.
Cuando en las ramas empiezan
los pájaros a cantar
y se desmaya la tarde
en las violetas del mar,
se pone blanca, con blanco
de una mejilla de sal.
Y cuando toca la noche
blando cuerno de metal
y las estrellas avanzan
mientras los aires se van,
en la raya de lo obscuro,
se comienza a deshojar.

Doña Rosita la soltera

[11] Era hermoso ginete,
y ahora montón de nieve.
Corrió ferias y montes
y brazos de mujeres.
Ahora, musgo de noche
le corona la frente.

Girasol de tu madre,
espejo de la tierra.
Que te pongan al pecho
cruz de amargas adelfas;
sábana que te cubra
de reluciente seda,
y el agua forme un llanto
entre tus manos quietas.

¡Ay, qué cuatro muchachos
llegan con hombros cansados!

¡Ay, qué cuatro galanes
traen a la muerte por el aire!

Vecinas.
                    Ya los traen.

Es lo mismo.
La cruz, la cruz.

Dulces clavos,
dulce cruz,
dulce nombre
de Jesús.

Que la cruz ampare a muertos y vivos.

Vecinas: con un cuchillo,
con un cuchillito,
en un dia señalado, entre las dos y las tres,
se mataron los dos hombres del amor.
Con un cuchillo,
con un cuchillito
que apenas cabe en la mano,
pero que penetra fino
por las carnes asombradas,
y que se para en el sitio
donde tiembla enmarañada
la obscura raíz del grito.

Y esto es un cuchillo,
un cuchillito

que apenas cabe en la mano;
pez sin escamas ni río,
para que un dia señalado, entre las dos y las tres,
con este cuchillo
se queden dos hombres duros
con los labios amarillos.

Y apenas cabe en la mano,
pero que penetra frío
por las carnes asombradas
y allí se para, en el sitio
donde tiembla enmarañada
la obscura raíz del grito.

Bodas de Sangre

[12]   ¡Ay, qué prado de pena!
¡Ay, qué puerta cerrada a la hermosura!,
que pido un hijo que sufrir, y el aire
me ofrece dalias de dormida luna.
Estos dos manantiales que yo tengo
de leche tibia son en la espesura
de mi carne dos pulsos de caballo
que hacen latir la rama de mi angustia.
¡Ay, pechos ciegos bajo mi vestido!
¡Ay, palomas sin ojos ni blancura!
¡Ay, qué dolor de sangre prisionera
me está clavando avispas en la nuca!
Pero tú has de venir, amor, mi niño,
porque el agua da sal, la tierra fruta,
y nuestro vientre guarda tiernos hijos,
como la nube lleva dulce lluvia.

Yerma

[13] En el arroyo frío
      lavo tu cinta.
      Como un jazmín caliente
      tienes la risa.
      Quiero vivir
      en la nevada chica
      de ese jazmín.

      ¡Ay de la casada seca!
      ¡Ay de la que tiene los pechos de arena!

      Dime si tu marido
      guarda semilla,
      para que el agua cante
      por tu camisa.
      . . . .
      Por el monte ya llega
      mi marido a comer.
      El me trae una rosa
      y yo le doy tres.

      Por el llano ya vino
      mi marido a cenar.
      Las brasas que me entrega
      cubro con arrayán.
      . . . .
      Hay que gemir en la sábana.

      ¡Y hay que cantar!

      Cuando el hombre nos trae
      la corona y el pan.

      Porque los brazos se enlazan.

Porque la luz se nos quiebra en la garganta.

Porque se endulza el tallo de las ramas.

Y las tiendas del viento cubren a las montañas.

Para que un niño funda
yertos vidrios del alba. . . .

Yerma

[14]   Señor, que florezca la rosa,
no me la dejéis en sombra.

Sobre su carne marchita
florezca la rosa amarilla.

Y en el vientre de tus siervas
la llama obscura de la tierra.
. . . .
¡Que diga a quién espera!

¡Que diga a quién aguarda!

¡Ay, con el vientre seco
y la color quebrada!

Cuando llegue la noche lo diré,
cuando llegue la noche clara.
Cuando llegue la noche de la romería
rasgaré los volantes de mi enagua.
. . . .
Si tú vienes a la romería

a pedir que tu vientre se abra,
no te pongas un velo de luto
sino dulce camisa de holanda.
Vete sola detrás de los muros
donde están las higueras cerradas
y soporta mi cuerpo de tierra
hasta el blanco gemido del alba.

. . . .

¡Dale ya con el cuerno!

¡Con la rosa y la danza!

¡Ay, cómo se cimbrea la casada!

. . . .

El cielo tiene jardines
con rosales de alegría,
entre rosal y rosal
la rosa de maravilla.

Yerma

[15]   El Cónsul pide bandeja
para los senos de Olalla.
Un chorro de venas verdes
le brota de la garganta.
Su sexo tiembla enredado
como un pájaro en las zarzas.
Por el suelo, ya sin norma,
brincan sus manos cortadas
que aun pueden cruzarse en tenue
oración decapitada.
Por los rojos agujeros
donde sus pechos estaban

se ven cielos diminutos
y arroyos de leche blanca.
Mil arbolillos de sangre
le cubren toda la espalda
y oponen húmedos troncos
al bisturí de las llamas.

. . . .

El Cónsul porta en bandeja
senos ahumados de Olalla.

Martirio de Santa Olalla

[16]   Tú sola vences la muerte;
vives palpando el hueco
de tu arrancada carne.
Una mano inmunda
desgarró tu costado;
rebanados los pechos,
se vió tu corazón desnudo.
La gangrena roía tus médulas;
agudos garfios arrebataron
tus entrañas a pedazos.

El Obispo leproso—GABRIEL MIRO

[17]   San Miguel, lleno de encajes
en la alcoba de su torre,
enseña sus bellos muslos
ceñidos por los faroles.

Arcángel domesticado
en el gesto de las doce,
finge una cólera dulce
de plumas y ruiseñores.
San Miguel canta en los vidrios;

efebo de tres mil noches,
fragante de agua colonia
y lejano de las flores.
. . . .

San Miguel se estaba quieto
en la alcoba de su torre,
con las enaguas cuajadas
de espejitos y entredoses.

San Miguel—Granada

[18]   Bajo el Moisés del incienso,
adormecida.

Ojos de toro te miraban.
Tu rosario llovía.

Con ese traje de profunda seda,
no te muevas, Virginia.

Da los negros melones de tus pechos
al rumor de la misa.

La soltera en misa

[19]   Un bello niño de junco,
anchos hombros, fino talle,
piel de nocturna manzana,
boca triste y ojos grandes,
nervio de plata caliente,
ronda la desierta calle.
Sus zapatos de charol
rompen las dalias del aire.
. . . .

Cuando la cabeza inclina
sobre su pecho de jaspe,
la noche busca llanuras
porque quiere arrodillarse.
. . . .
—San Gabriel: el niño llora
en el vientre de su madre.
No olvides que los gitanos
te regalaron el traje.

Anunciación de los Reyes,
bien lunada y mal vestida,
abre la puerta al lucero
que por la calle venía.
El Arcángel San Gabriel,
entre azucena y sonrisa,
biznieto de la Giralda,
se acercaba de visita.
En su chaleco bordado
grillos ocultos palpitan.
Las estrellas de la noche
se volvieron campanillas.

—San Gabriel: Aquí me tienes
con tres clavos de alegría.
Tu fulgor abre jazmines
sobre mi cara encendida.
. . . .
—Dios te salve, Anunciación,
bien lunada y mal vestida.
Tu niño tendrá en el pecho
un lunar y tres heridas.

—¡Ay, San Gabriel que reluces!
¡Gabrielillo de mi vida!
En el fondo de mis pechos
ya nace la leche tibia.

—Dios te salve, Anunciación.
Madre de cien dinastías.
Áridos lucen tus ojos
paisajes de caballista.

San Gabriel—Sevilla

[20] Silencio de cal y mirto.
Malvas en las hierbas finas.
La monja borda alhelíes
sobre una tela pajiza.
Vuelan en la araña gris
siete pájaros del prisma.
La iglesia gruñe a lo lejos
como un oso panza arriba.
¡Qué bien borda! ¡Con qué gracia!
Sobre la tela pajiza
ella quisiera bordar
flores de su fantasía.
. . . .
Cinco toronjas se endulzan
en la cercana cocina.
Las cinco llagas de Cristo
cortadas en Almería.
Por los ojos de la monja
galopan dos caballistas.
Un rumor último y sordo
le despega la camisa,
y, al mirar nubes y montes

en las yertas lejanías,
se quiebra su corazón
de azucar y yerbaluisa.
¡Oh, qué llanura empinada
con veinte soles arriba!
¡Qué ríos puestos de pié
vislumbra su fantasía!
Pero sigue con sus flores. . . .

La monja gitana

[21]   Su luna de pergamino
Preciosa tocando viene.
Al verla se ha levantado
el viento que nunca duerme.
San Cristobalón desnudo,
lleno de lenguas celestes,
mira a la niña tocando
una dulce gaita ausente.
—Niña, deja que levante
tu vestido para verte.
Abre en mis dedos antiguos
la rosa azul de tu vientre.

Preciosa tira el pandero
y corre sin detenerse.
El viento-hombrón la persigue
con una espada caliente.
. . . .
¡Preciosa, corre, Preciosa,
que te coge el viento verde!
¡Preciosa, corre, Preciosa!
¡Míralo por donde viene!
Sátiro de estrellas bajas

con sus lenguas relucientes.
Preciosa, llena de miedo,
entra en la casa que tiene,
más arriba de los pinos,
el cónsul de los ingleses.
. . . .
El inglés da a la gitana
un vaso de tibia leche
y una copa de ginebra
que Preciosa no se bebe.

Y mientras cuenta, llorando,
su aventura a aquella gente,
en las tejas de pizarra
el viento, furioso, muerde.

En los picos de la Sierra
los carabineros duermen
guardando las blancas torres
donde viven los ingleses.

Preciosa y el aire

[22]   La luna gira en el cielo
sobre las tierras sin agua.
. . . .
Thamar estaba soñando
pájaros en su garganta,
al son de panderos fríos
y cítaras enlunadas.
. . . .
Amnón, delgado y concreto,
en la torre la miraba,

llenas las ingles de espuma
y oscilaciones la barba.
. . . .
Amnón estaba mirando
la luna redonda y baja,
y vió en la luna los pechos
durísimos de su hermana.
. . . .
Linfa de pozo oprimida
brota silencio en las jarras.
En el musgo de los troncos
la cobra tendida canta.
Amnón gime por la tela
fresquísima de la cama.
Yedra del escalofrío
cubre su carne quemada.
Thamar entra silenciosa
en la alcoba silenciada.
. . . .
—Thamar, en tus pechos altos
hay dos peces que me llaman,
y en las yemas de tus dedos
rumor de rosa encerrada.

Los cien caballos del rey
en el patio relinchaban.
. . . .
Ya la coge del cabello,
ya la camisa la rasga. . . .
Corales tibios dibujan
arroyos en rubio mapa.

Thamar y Amnón

[23] Y que yo me la llevé al rio
creyendo que era mozuela,
pero tenía marido.

Fué la noche de Santiago
y casi por compromiso.
Se apagaron los faroles
y se encendieron los grillos.
En las últimas esquinas
toqué sus pechos dormidos,
y se me abrieron de pronto
como ramos de jacintos.
El almidón de su enagua
me sonaba en el oído
como una pieza de seda
rasgada por diez cuchillos.

Sin luz de plata en sus copas
los árboles han crecido,
y un horizonte de perros
ladra muy lejos del río.
. . . .
Sus muslos se me escapaban
como peces sorprendidos,
la mitad llenos de lumbre,
la mitad llenos de frío.
Aquella noche corrí
el mejor de los caminos,
montado en potra de nácar
sin bridas y sin estribos.
No quiero decir, por hombre,
las cosas que ella me dijo.
. . . .

Me porté como quien soy.
Como un gitano legítimo.
La regalé un costurero
grande, de raso pajizo,
y no quise enamorarme
porque teniendo marido
me dijo que era mozuela
cuando la llevaba al río.

La casada infiel

[23 cont.]

Ni nardos ni caracolas
tienen el cutis tan fino,
ni los cristales con luna
relumbran con ese brillo.

La casada infiel

[24]   Se le vió caminar solo con Ella,
sin miedo a su guadaña.
—Ya el sol en torre y torre; los martillos
en yunque—yunque y yunque de la fraguas.
Hablaba Federico,
requebrando a la Muerte. Ella escuchaba.
Porque ayer en mi verso, compañera,
sonaba el golpe de tus secas palmas,
y diste el hielo a mi cantar, y el filo
a mi tragedia de tu hoz de plata;
ye cantaré la carne que no tienes,
los ojos que te faltan,
tus cabellos que el viento sacudía,
los rojos labios donde te besaban. . . .
Hoy como ayer, gitana, muerte mía,

qué bien contigo a solas,
Por estos aires de Granada, mi Granada.

El crimen fué en Granada—Canto II

—ANTONIO MACHADO

[25]   Todo lo vivo que pasa
              por las puertas de la Muerte
              va con la cabeza baja
              y un aire blanco durmiente
              . . . .
              cubierto con el silencio
              que es el manto de la Muerte.
              . . . .
              Y mi sangre sobre el campo
              sea rosado y dulce limo
              donde claven sus azadas
              los cansados campesinos.

                                        Cigarra

[26]   Cantan los niños
              en la noche quieta:
              ¡Arroyo claro,
              fuente serena!

Los niños: ¿Qué tiene tu divino
              corazón de fiesta?

Yo: Un doblar de campanas
              perdidas en la niebla.

Los niños: Ya nos dejas cantando
              en la plazuela.

¡Arroyo claro,
fuente serena!
. . . .
¿Qué sientes en tu boca
roja y sedienta?

Yo: El sabor de los huesos
de mi gran calavera.

Los niños: Bebe el agua tranquila
de la canción añeja.
¡Arroyo claro,
fuente serena!

¿Por qué te vas tan lejos
de la plazuela?

Yo: Se ha llenado de luces
mi corazón de seda,
de campanas perdidas,
de lirios y de abejas.
Y yo me iré muy lejos,
más allá.de esas sierras.
Más allá de los mares,
cerca de las estrellas.
Para pedirle a Cristo
Señor que me devuelva
mi alma antigua de niño,
madura de leyendas,
con el gorro de plumas
y el sable de madera.

Balada de la placeta

[27] No hay nadie que al dar un beso
no sienta la sonrisa de la gente sin rostro,
ni nadie que al tocar un recién nacido
olvide las inmóviles calaveras de caballo.

Porque las rosas buscan en la frente
un duro paisaje de hueso
y las manos del hombre no tienen más sentido
que imitar a las raíces bajo tierra.

Como me pierdo en el corazón de algunos niños
me he perdido muchas veces por el mar.
Ignorante del agua voy buscando
una muerte de luz que me consuma.

Casida de la muerte clara

[28] Quiero dormir el sueño de las manzanas,
alejarme del tumulto de los cementerios,
quiero dormir el sueño de aquel niño
que se quería cortar el corazón en alta mar.

No quiero que me repita que los muertos no pierden
la sangre,
que la boca podrida sigue pidiendo agua;
no quiero enterarme de los martirios de la hierba
ni de la luna con boca de serpiente
que trabaja antes del amanecer.

Casida de la huida

[29] Vengo a buscar lo que busco,
mi alegría y mi persona.
. . . .
No me recuerdes el mar

que la pena negra brota
en las tierras de aceituna
bajo el rumor de las hojas.

. . . .

¡Oh pena de los gitanos!
Pena limpia y siempre sola.
¡Oh pena de cauce oculto
y madrugada remota!

Romance de la pena negra

[30]   —Ya puedes cortar, si gustas,
las adelfas de tu patio.
Pinta una cruz en la puerta
y pon tu nombre debajo,
porque cicutas y ortigas
nacerán en tu costado,
y agujas de cal mojada
te morderán los zapatos.

. . . .

El veinticinco de junio
abrió sus ojos Amargo,
y el veinticinco de agosto
se tendió para cerrarlos.
Hombres bajaban la calle
para ver al emplazado,
que fijaba sobre el muro
su soledad con descanso.
Y la sábana impecable,
de duro acento romano,
daba equilibrio a la muerte
con las rectas de sus paños.

Romance del emplazado

[31] —Compadre, quiero morir
decentemente en mi cama.
De acero, si puede ser,
con las sábanas de holanda.

Romance sonámbulo

[32] Limoncito amarillo,
limonero,
Echad los limoncitos
al viento.
¡Ya lo sabéis! . . . Porque luego,
luego,
un velón y una manta
en el suelo.

Lamentación de la muerte

[33] A la mitad del camino
cortó limones redondos
y los fué tirando al agua
hasta que la puso de oro.
. . . .
—Antonio, ¿quién eres tú?
Si te llamaras Camborio
hubieras hecho una fuente
de sangre con cinco chorros.
Ni tú eres hijo de nadie,
ni legítimo Camborio.
¡Se acabaron los gitanos
que iban por el monte solos!
Están los viejos cuchillos
tiritando bajo el polvo.

Prendimiento de Antoñito el Camborio

[34]   Voces de muerte sonaron
        cerca del Guadalquivir.
        Voces antiguas que cercan
        voz de clavel varonil.
        Les clavó sobre las botas
        mordiscos de jabalí.
        En la lucha daba saltos
        jabonados de delfín.
        Bañó con sangre enemiga
        su corbata carmesí,
        pero eran cuatro puñales
        y tuvo que sucumbir.
        . . . .
        Tres golpes de sangre tuvo
        y se murió de perfil.
        Viva moneda que nunca
        se volverá a repetir.
        Un angel marchoso pone
        su cabea en un cojín.
        Otros de rubor cansado
        encendieron un candil.

                Muerte de Antoñito el Camborio

[35]   Muerto se quedó en la calle
        con un puñal en el pecho.
        No lo conocía nadie.
        ¡Cómo temblaba el farol!
        Madre.
        ¡Cómo temblaba el farolito
        de la calle!
        Era madrugada. Nadie
        pudo asomarse a sus ojos
        abiertos al duro aire.

Que muerto se quedó en la calle,
que con un puñal en el pecho,
y que no lo conocía nadie.

Sorpresa

[36]   Tierra
              vieja
              del candil
              y la pena.
              Tierra
              de las hondas cisternas.

              Tierra
              de la muerte sin ojos
              y las flechas.

Tierra seca

[37]   Temblaban en los tejados
              farolillos de hojalata.
              Mil panderos de cristal
              herían la madrugada.
              . . . .
              El largo viento dejaba
              en la boca un raro gusto
              de hiel, de menta y de albahaca.

Romance sonámbulo

[38] La aurora llega y nadie la recibe en su boca
porque alli no hay mañana ni esperanza posible.
A veces las monedas en enjambres furiosos
taladran y devoran abandonados niños.

Los primeros que salen comprenden con sus huesos
que no habrá paraíso ni amores deshojados;

saben que van al cieno de números y leyes,
a los juegos sin arte, a sudores sin fruto.

La luz es sepultada por cadenas y ruidos
en impúdico reto de ciencia sin raíces.
Por los barrios hay gentes que vacilan insomnes
como recién salidas de un naufragio de sangre.

Poeta en Nueva York—La aurora

[39] Aquellos ojos míos de mil novecientos diez
no vieron enterrar a los muertos,
ni la feria de ceniza del que llora por la madrugada,
ni el corazón que tiembla arrinconado como un
caballito del mar.

. . . .

y una luna incomprensible que iluminaba por los
rincones
los pedazos de limón seco bajo el negro duro de las
botellas.

. . . .

Aquellos ojos míos en el cuello de la jaca,
en el seno traspasado de Santa Rosa dormida,
en los tejados del amor, con gemidos y frescas
manos,
en un jardín donde los gatos se comían a las ranas.

. . . .

No preguntarme nada. He visto que las cosas
cuando buscan su curso encuentran su vacío.
Hay un dolor de huecos por el aire sin gente
y en mis ojos criaturas vestidas ¡sin desnudo!

Poeta en Nueva York—Intermedio

[40] Quiero llorar porque me da la gana,
      como lloran los niños del último banco,
      porque yo no soy un hombre, ni un poeta, ni una
          hoja,
      pero si un pulso herido que sonda las cosas del otro
          lado.

                              Poeta en Nueva York—
                              Poema doble del lago Edem

[41] Más vale sollozar afilando la navaja
      o asesinar a los perros en las alucinantes cacerías
      que resistir en la madrugada
      los interminables trenes de leche,
      los interminables trenes de sangre,
      y los trenes de rosas maniatadas
      por los comerciantes de perfumes.
      · · · ·
      Todos los días se matan en Nueva York
      cuatro millones de patos,
      cinco millones de cerdos,
      dos mil palomas para el gusto de los agonizantes.
      · · · ·
      ¿Qué voy a hacer? ¿Ordenar los paisajes?
      ¿Ordenar los amores que luego son fotografias,
      que luego son pedazos de madera y bocanadas de
          sangre?
      No, no; yo denuncio,
      yo denuncio la conjura
      de estas desiertas oficinas
      que no radian las agonías. · · ·

                              Poeta en Nueva York—
                              New York, oficina y denuncia

[42] Con una cuchara
      arrancaba los ojos a los cocdrilos
      y golpeaba el trasero de los monos.
      Con una cuchara.
      . . . .
      ¡Ay, Harlem! ¡Ay, Harlem!
      No hay angustia comparable a tus rojos oprimidos,
      a tu sangre estremecida dentro del eclipse obscuro,
      a tu violencia granate sordomuda en la penumbra,
      a tu gran rey prisionero, con un traje de conserje.
      . . . .
      Negros, Negros, Negros, Negros.

      La sangre no tiene puertas en vuestra noche boca
         arriba.
      No hay rubor. Sangre furiosa por debajo de las
         pieles,
      viva en la espina del puñal. . . .
      . . . .
      Es la sangre que viene, que vendrá
      por los tejados y azoteas, por todas partes,
      para quemar la clorofilia de las mujeres rubias,
      para gemir al pié de las camas ante el insomnio de
         los lavabos.
      Y estrellarse en una aurora de tabaco y bajo ama-
         rillo.
      . . . .
      Negros, Negros, Negros, Negros.

      Jamás sierpe, ni cebra, ni mula
      palidecieron al morir.
      El leñador no sabe cuando expiran
      los clamorosos árboles que corta.

Aguardad bajo la sombra vegetal de vuestro rey
a que cicutas y cardos y ortigas turben postreras
azoteas.
Entonces, negros, entonces, entonces, . . .
Poeta en Nueva York—El Rey de Harlem

[43] Que ya las cobras silbarán por los ultimos pisos,
que ya las ortigas estremecerán patios y terrazas,
que ya la Bolsa será una pirámide de musgo,
que ya vendrán lianas después de los fusiles
y muy pronto, muy pronto, muy pronto.
¡Ay, Wall Street!
Poeta en Nueva York—Danza de la Muerte

[44] . . . los negros que sacan las escupideras,
los muchachos que tiemblan bajo el terror pálido
de los directores,
las mujeres ahogadas en aceites minerales,
la muchedumbre de martillo, de violín o de nube,
. . . .
ha de gritar con voz tan desgarrada
hasta que las ciudades tiemblen como niñas
y rompan las prisiones del aceite y de la música,
porque queremos el pan nuestro de cada día. . . .
Poeta en Nueva York—Grito hacia Roma

[45] A las cinco de la tarde.
Eran las cinco en punto de la tarde.
Un niño trajo la blanca sábana
a las cinco de la tarde.
Una espuerta de cal ya prevenida
a las cinco de la tarde.
Lo demás era muerte y solo muerte

a las cinco de la tarde.

. . . .

Cuando el sudor de nieve fué llegando
a las cinco de la tarde,
cuando la plaza se cubrió de yodo
a las cinco de la tarde,
la muerte puso huevos en la herida
a las cinco de la tarde.
A las cinco de la tarde.
A las cinco en punto de la tarde.

Llanto por Ignacio Sanchez Mejías

[46]   ¡Que no quiero verla!

Dile a la luna que venga,
que no quiero ver la sangre
de Ignacio sobre la arena.

¡Que no quiero verla!

La luna de par en par.
Caballo de nubes quietas,
y la plaza gris del sueño
con sauces en las barreras.
¡Que no quiero verla!
Que mi recuerdo se quema.
¡Avisad a los jazmines
con su blancura pequeña!
¡Que no quiero verla!

La vaca del viejo mundo
pasaba su triste lengua
sobre un hocico de sangres

derramadas en la arena.
. . . .
¡Que no quiero verla!

Por las gradas sube Ignacio
con toda su muerte a cuestas.
Buscaba el amanecer,
y el amanecer no era.
Busca su perfil seguro,
y el sueño lo desorienta.
Buscaba su hermoso cuerpo
y encontró su sangre abierta.
¡No me digáis que la vea!
. . . .
No se cerraron sus ojos
cuando vió los cuernos cerca,
pero las madres terribles
levantaron la cabeza.
Y a través de las ganaderías,
hubo un aire de voces secretas
que gritaban a toros celestes,
mayorales de pálida niebla.
. . . .
Pero ya duerme sin fín.
Ya los musgos y la hierba
abren con dedos seguros
la flor de su calavera.
Y su sangre ya viene cantando;
cantando por marismas y praderas,
resbalando por cuernos ateridos,
vacilando sin alma por la niebla,
tropezando con miles de pezuñas

como una larga, obscura, triste lengua,
para formar un charco de agonía
junto al Guadalquivir de las estrellas.
¡Oh blanco muro de España!
¡Oh negro toro de pena!
¡Oh sangre dura de Ignacio!
¡Oh ruiseñor de sus venas!
No.
¡Que no quiero verla!
Que no hay cáliz que la contenga,
que no hay golondrinas que se la beban,
no hay escarcha de luz que la enfríe,
no hay canto ni diluvio de azucenas,
no hay cristal que la cubra de plata.
No.
¡¡Yo no quiero verla!!

Llanto por Ignacio Sanchez Mejías

[47] Ya está sobre la piedra Ignacio el bien nacido.
Ya se acabó; ¿qué pasa? Contemplad su figura:
la muerte le ha cubierto de pálidos azufres
y le ha puesto cabeza de obscuro minotauro.
. . . .
¿Qué dicen? Un silencio con hedores reposa.
Estamos con un cuerpo presente que se esfuma,
con una forma clara que tuvo ruiseñores
y la vemos llenarse de agujeros sin fondo.
. . . .
Yo quiero ver aquí los hombres de voz dura.
Los que doman caballos y dominan los ríos;
los hombres que les suena el esqueleto y cantan
con una boca llena de sol y pedernales.

Aquí quiero yo verlos. Delante de la piedra.
Delante de este cuerpo con las riendas quebradas.
Yo quiero que me enseñen donde está la salida
para este capitán atado por la muerte.

. . . .

No quiero que le tapen la cara con pañuelos
para que se acostumbre con la muerte que lleva.
Vete, Ignacio: No sientas el caliente bramido.
Duerme, vela, reposa: ¡Tambien se muere el mar!

Llanto por Ignacio Sanchez Mejías

[48]   No te conoce el toro ni la higuera,
ni caballos ni hormigas de tu casa.
No te conoce el niño ni la tarde
porque te has muerto para siempre.

. . . .

El otoño vendrá con caracolas,
uva de niebla y montes agrupados,
pero nadie querrá mirar tus ojos
porque te has muerto para siempre.

Porque te has muerto para siempre,
como todos los muertos de la Tierra,
como todos los muertos que se olvidan
en un montón de perros apagados.

No te conoce nadie. No. Pero yo te canto.
Yo canto para luego tu perfil y tu gracia.
La madurez insigne de tu conocimiento.
Tu apetencia de muerte y el gusto de su boca.
La tristeza que tuvo tu valiente alegría.

Llanto por Ignacio Sanchez Mejías

[49] Vivo estabas, Dios mío, dentro del ostensorio.
Punzado por tu Padre con agujas de lumbre.
Latiendo como el pobre corazón de la rana
que los médicos ponen en el frasco de vidrio.

. . . .

Es así, Dios andado, como quiero tenerte,
panderito de harina para el recien nacido.

Oda al Santísimo Sacramento del altar

[50]   Los densos bueyes del agua
embisten a los muchachos
que se bañan en las lunas
de sus cuernos ondulados.

. . . .

Será de noche, en lo obscuro,
por los montes imantados,
donde los bueyes del agua
beben los juncos soñando.

Romance del emplazado

[51] *   Verde que te quiero verde.
Verde viento. Verdes ramas.
El barco sobre la mar
y el caballo en la montaña.

. . . .

Bajo la luna gitana
las cosas la están mirando
y ella no puede mirarlas.

. . . .

* Please note that the order of quotations in the English translations of this poem (pp. 128 to 130) are different from the original
Spanish version as given above. This is because the passages in question are quoted arbitrarily in connection with the analysis.

Verde que te quiero verde.
Grandes estrellas de escarcha
vienen con el pez de sombra
que abre el camino del alba
La higuera frota su vientre
con la lija de sus ramas,
y el monte, gato garduño,
eriza sus pitas agrias.
. . . .
—Trescientas rosas morenas
lleva tu pechera blanca.
Tu sangre rezuma y huele
alrededor de tu faja.
Pero yo ya no soy yo,
ni mi casa es ya mi casa.
. . . .
Un carámbano de luna
la sostiene sobre el agua.
Guardias civiles borrachos
en la puerta golpeaban.
Verde que te quiero verde.
Verde viento. Verdes ramas.
El barco sobre la mar.
Y el caballo en la montaña.

                          Romance sonámbulo